Joan of Arc

In Light of Anthroposophy & Spiritual Science

By Bradford Judson

Send inquiries to joanofarcbook2022@outlook.com.

This is a self-published work. All images used in this publication are public domain or were photographed directly by the author and are free for commercial and personal use.

ISBN: 978-0-9990054-1-5

---

[1] Steiner, Rudolf. On Chaos and Cosmos. GA284. "Nowadays lawsuits are enacted against the stealing of thoughts, of the spiritual property of others. Lawsuits against plagiarism were never instituted by the Rosicrucians. They did not mind what the personal source was from which such things went out; the main thing was that they came into the world. It is a vicious custom of our time to institute legal proceedings against the stealing of thoughts."

Table of Contents

"La-Pucelle!", Circa-1907, by Frank-Craig (1874-1918). The full-sized image has been cropped.

Acknowledgments

I dedicate this work to Christ-Jesus who perpetually loves, leads, guides, helps, influences, and informs humanity. The Initiate of Initiates is our elder brother, redeemer, advocate, representative, friend, and life-guide. He knows all, loves all, and sees all. I further dedicate this work to our Holy Mother and Michaél, the Archangel of the Sun, as the bringer of transformation, courage, light, knowledge, and balance.

I also dedicate this work to...

∞ The Great Initiates and leaders of humanity. This includes Christian Rosenkreuz, or Lazarus-John, the Knight of the Rose Cross and founder of Rosicrucianism, and Rudolf Steiner the founder of Anthroposophy and those who carried on his work. They are dedicated to the progress of the individual human being through transformation, freedom, and a greater understanding of, and relationship with, the Christ and Michael in each person.

∞ The light-bearers, initiates, and spirit-guides whose names are mostly unknown to us in this life who are forever committed to humanity's long journey to freedom, redemption, unity, and civility.

∞ The spiritual guides who inspired this work and helped me to bring it to proper completion.

∞ My loving, compassionate, and dedicated parents who provided me with a happy childhood and a good life. I acknowledge my father, who now resides in the spiritual world, whose guidance has helped me significantly. He has revealed many spiritual insights, connections, ideas, and experiences to me since his transition.

∞ All of my pet friends who have helped me over the course of my life. Most recently, it was Henry the Maltipoo who left me too soon. He is a clever, intuitive, brave, and gentle little being who touched me to the depths of my heart.

Introduction

Since the death of Joan of Arc, thousands of books, articles, and studies have been published on the life of Joan of Arc. One analysis concluded that Joan was one of the top 5 people written about in human history. Few people in history have garnered as much attention as Joan. The mystery of her life and death (born January 6, 1412, died May 30, 1431)[2] has compelled countless scholars, theologians, writers, historians, and people of simple faith alike over the centuries to examine her life and contemplate the miraculous nature of her accomplishments and martyrdom.[3] It is also true, however, that while so much historical research has been conducted on the Maid of Lorraine, much of which is insightful and well-written, not much new information has come to light. Naturally, any historical study of Joan is based on the limitations of information available through surviving documents, letters, and testimony by those who knew her. Most biographies are lists of historical events, descriptions of Joan's accomplishments, and quotes. Some studies have explored hypotheses on certain dogmatic aspects that have no historical value.[4] Therefore, it is impossible to gain anything but a partial and imperfect view of her life, and one is left to speculation.

Thus, a disparity emerges regarding the true substance of Joan's mission from a perspective of objective spiritual facts. Understanding Joan's true mission is simply not feasible in any traditional, or exoteric, study where

---

[2] Historically, Joan's birth is found in a letter written by a certain Lord Perceval de Boulainvilliers to the Duke of Milan on July 21, 1429. The relevant passage reads: "On the night of the Epiphany of Our Lord (January 6) ...she entered mortal life..." It was later confirmed by Dr. Rudolf Steiner, which shall be discussed throughout this work.

[3] Joan's name is synonymous with the Maid of Orléans, the Maid of Lorraine, the Maid, Jeannette, Jeanne, Johanna, Jehanne, and other derivations. She signed her name "Johanna". The name Joan, or Jeanne, is the French feminine equivalent of the English name John. Due to Joan's historic and spiritual mission and its genuine connection to the mission and task of St. John, there is a spiritual a common task between the two people as leaders that extends beyond a mere name. The individuality once known as Lazarus later took on the name of John who wrote the Gospel of John and the Book of Revelation. Rudolf Steiner referred to him as "Lazarus-John" and he appears again and again throughout human history as a great leader of humanity. Lazarus-John's mission is one of special significance and he has helped to bring about a unique path in the world into the West. Refer to the Gospel of St. John and the Christian Rosenkreutz lectures by Rudolf Steiner for more information.

[4] One such historical hypothesis is that Joan's family was of in the French royal bloodline, which is not provable and is essentially unimportant.

outer aspects of history are contemplated. This is because most people have yet to be exposed to a foundational and mature approach to the spiritual sciences that enable such a study. While traditional studies enable one towards knowledge, religious texts, opinions, hypotheses, and dogma, a lot of which are based on bias or other limitations, we inevitably fall short of piercing the greater mystery of Joan's life. As a part of my task in this life, I have chosen to bridge that gap as a life-mission as best that I can.

My quest, experience, and the results of my spiritual and historical research have revealed that there is another source of information that has been largely overlooked in modern times regarding history and in particular Joan's life. These insights can only be perceived, and communicated, by one who has effectively bridged the gap between the limitations of the intellect and the higher spiritual self, thus building and maintaining a mature bridge to the spiritual worlds. It is only through this path, which is the path of the spiritual initiate, that one can truly embark on a journey into a deeper study of Joan's life and perceive the significance of her mission and accomplishment. So, we must seek out one who successfully constructed a genuine spiritual bridge, acquired information regarding Joan's life from a reliable and comprehensive source of information in the spiritual worlds, and chose to reveal certain facts to the public in an understandable way...

There is, although it is unknown to the majority of people today, another dimension of historical research that will emerge in the future and it is imprinted upon the ethers, or finest substance, of the spiritual worlds of which humanity is an integrated aspect. It is, perhaps, more appropriate to refer to this form of research as spiritual-historical research. This form of research is based on an expanded spiritual perception, capability, and faculty inherent within the human being that, if sufficiently developed, can reveal true insights about the past, historical personalities, cultures, events, the cosmos, the divine beings who oversee humanity's evolution, and the true nature of the human being. These are the mysteries. They are the sphere of activity of the spiritual initiate; the mature and transformed human being who has purged his or her lower impulses and unlocked the mystery of the human spirit within themselves. Historically they have been called by many names including initiates, saints, mystics, and hierophants. All of these terms, while valid, are ambiguous and fail to grasp what a spiritual initiate truly is. It is a foreign concept in today's world as the mysteries, or those formal training facilities in the ancient world that taught and preserved a valid path to spiritual unfolding, have faded into obscurity over time. The substance of life, and indeed the path of spiritual initiation, is soul transformation. One aspect of this transformation is that individuals can, in a conscious way, look back upon the world in an objective way having the ability to rise above the confines of the physical world.

So, where do we find such a person? In actuality, these individuals live amongst us today but very few lead public lives. Fortunately, one came to us with the mission of helping humanity through a higher mission. A man incarnated in the late 19th century who brought a path, and a task, forward to humanity to achieve spiritual transformation. Dr. Rudolf Steiner (1861-1925) dedicated his life to this mission and made great sacrifices along the way over long periods of time. During the course of his life, he delivered thousands of lectures and wrote many books and articles where he revealed the results of his spiritual-historical research for others to learn from and therefore grow themselves as individuals. His research included previously unknown aspects of certain historical personalities including Joan of Arc.

With this work, I have chosen to integrate a historical aspect to Joan's remarkable life and, alongside it, provide insights from the archives of Dr. Rudolf Steiner's lectures, books, and articles written over the course of his life. He gave the name "Anthroposophy"[5] and "Spiritual Science" to his movement so that each individual could become objective and active students of the spiritual worlds and how we, as human beings, are connected. Therefore, I have chosen to refer to Steiner's published observations on Joan's life as has been translated into English. Each chapter in this imperfect study will address aspects of Joan's life in this way; historical facts as accepted by traditional research and spiritual facts as revealed by Dr. Steiner. In this way, and only in this way, can something of the global importance of Joan's mission be brought to light so that researchers and students of Joan can begin to form an appreciation for what she contributed not just for France, but also England, Europe, and the world.

Today's view of history attributes the world of phenomena to chance, choice, luck, or egotism and it necessarily disregards the deeper aspects of the human soul and destiny. Individuals like Joan emerge at critical points

---

[5] "Anthro" meaning the human being and "Sophy", or "Sophia", meaning wisdom.

of history as a result of spiritual influences, destiny, and a mission that affects large groups of people. They seem to appear out of nowhere at just the right propitious moment. Joan, and those who share a common task of a similar nature, come into the world to make a larger contribution to humanity, the substance of which is invisible to the masses. Some people, however, can discern this deeper significance of these people's lives, even if it is just vaguely. A perception of the nature of the special mission of people like Joan typically only occurs years, decades, and centuries after their task has been accomplished.

The true facts of history are accessible to those who can perceive them through a valid process and expanded perception. The spiritual facts regarding Joan's life as revealed by Dr. Steiner are not based on hypothesis, speculation, or theory. This knowledge is predicated upon a deeper wisdom and mature perception that is achieved only through a genuine supersensible and expanded faculty. This capability is the product of the path of expedited spiritual development that allows one to acquire and relay, as is appropriate, what is perceived. This expanded capability of spiritual-historical research, which is the result of a mature form of human transformation that occurs only over long periods of time and effort, extends far beyond the inherited and developed intellectual boundaries of the average human being regardless of one's education.

There are reasons why human beings do not possess inherent abilities to perceive the deeper aspects of the world, including Joan's mission, at our current stage of evolution one of which are the conditions of the age in which we live that are subject to certain influences that we are not aware of. The second cause is that one must seek out this ability and skillset and diligently cultivate it over long periods of time through committed effort and training. The materialistic influences of our age have created an over-reliance on the purely materialistic observations of the intellect. This over-reliance on the purely intellectual analysis that is devoid of inner insights that disregard the soul and the spirit of the human being and our relationship to the spiritual worlds, has blotted out a bridge to objective spiritual and intuitive knowledge which, in actuality, is accessible to anyone. When one sets out on the path, as it were, and eventually achieves an inner transformation gradually, step by step, over time. The difficult and long path is referred to in esoteric spiritual sciences, and the mysteries, as Initiation. On the Christ path, as brought forth in the Middle Ages through the tales of Parsifal and King Arthur, spiritual initiation is properly viewed in light of the Quest for the Holy Grail.

Steiner's lectures and writings are available online and in print and there are vast amounts of information available to a student of the spiritual mysteries. One could never exhaust the volumes of material written by Steiner and those who followed in his footsteps and helped to found the Anthroposophical Society. In relatively quick time, especially compared to the days when the written word was available only through significant effort and manual means, we can simply use an online search mechanism and read through thousands of books, lectures, and writings at lightning speeds. We should be grateful to people like Dr. Steiner who dedicated his life to the task of revealing, as a part of his life mission and destiny, as much of the hidden elements of the spiritual worlds and the hidden nature of humanity's existence as was appropriate and feasible during his life.[6]

A man of remarkable endurance, Dr. Steiner gave an estimated 5,000 lectures over the span of some 37 years throughout Europe. Steiner's complete works comprise some 330 volumes. His works have been translated into at least 100 languages. Over the course of his life, he lectured and wrote on many topics including the various relationships of higher beings and the dimensions of the spiritual worlds, humanity's history, karmic relationships, farming, medicine, a spiritual path of development, and education that were based on the true nature of the human being gathered through his expanded and mature spiritual faculties.

Amongst the many individuals he chose to consider and discuss publicly were some, but not all, insights of Jeanne d'Arc and the far-reaching importance of her life and martyrdom and how it shaped the destiny of Western Europe and the world. To my knowledge, there have been no other genuine researchers who have come forward publicly to provide genuine insights into the true nature and circumstances of Joan's life to the world in light of true spiritual facts as did Dr. Steiner. Therefore, his research is critical to the construction of this study and serves as the foundation stone upon which valid esoteric, or spiritual, observations are

---

[6] Many, but not all, of Steiner's lectures and written materials are available for free on www.rsarchive.org. Many of his lectures are also available as free audio books. We should also be grateful to those who are committed to digitizing and sharing Steiner's works and making them available for free online. Refer to www.rsarchive.org for a free online search tool of Steiner's body of knowledge.

made. Given Steiner's task and the ethical boundaries of historical research in a spiritual context, he revealed only as much as was appropriate for his task, the moment, and the mission of the movement to bring the reality of the spiritual worlds to the general public. There is an ethical boundary where private details, especially regarding certain details of an individual's life, should not be revealed to the general public. Therefore, as is the case with this study, I refer to Steiner's lectures and commentaries that were delivered in public venues during the course of his life.

Without the knowledge that can only be acquired through genuine and mature spiritual insights, clairvoyance, and faculties nothing of the far-reaching nature of Joan of Arc's mission and martyrdom would be known to the world outside of the exoteric aspects. If we rely solely on that knowledge, a researcher inevitably falls short of grasping Joan's global importance. As with all things, students of Joan are conflicted. Without any genuine insights, some people believe that Joan's voices and visions were the results of genuine spiritual communications of Angels and spiritual guides and that she was on a divine mission. Conversely, others, in their blindness, egotism, or personal bias against the concept of spiritual experience, have attributed Joan's visions and voices to mental illness.[7] Regardless of one's perspective, if one employs a purely materialistic approach to the study of an individual like Joan who led a world-historic destiny, the most important elements are obscured and remain a mystery. This study is a combination of generally accepted facts gathered from historical documents that are readily available, including excerpts from the translations of surviving transcripts of both of Joan's trials, and Steiner's spiritual insights that provide the crux of the value of this work.

The perpetual questions that linger around Joan's life, and mission, perhaps will come into better clarity with this study when one considers the actual spiritual realities behind the situation in France and why events unfolded that required the intervention of higher beings who worked through the Maid of Lorraine. After all, in light of historical events have not countries, such as France, been absorbed, conquered, or permanently altered during periods of military conflict over the course of human

---

[7] There has been a shift in the 20th century from the attribution of Joan's faculties from that of witchcraft, sorcery, and devil worship during her life to that of mental illness in the 20th and 21st centuries. This is a byproduct of materialism and the age in which we live that disregards the possibility, and reality, of genuine spiritual perception and experience.

history? Why was it so important at that particular moment in history that a simple farm woman be raised, as aided and guided by spiritual guardians, to liberate and redeem France from the English and Burgundian nations? What are the spiritual facts behind the reality that an uneducated, virtuous, brave, and good-natured girl whom the French armies to victory during one of the most turbulent and chaotic centuries of the medieval period?

It is my sincere hope this study brings value to the reader's spiritual and historical research regarding this pivotal time history and the role of one who took on a critical, difficult, and sacrificial task for the sake of France, England, Europe, the world, and thus humanity.

Bradford Judson
January 6, 2022

Prelude

What is known through traditional historical documents about the life of Joan of Arc is sufficient to gain an exoteric, and partial, picture of her life. Traditionally, her role is viewed from a one-sided perspective as a heroine of French liberty. We know from historical records that Joan was an uneducated farm woman born in France during the chaos of the Hundred Years' War when England, Burgundy, and France were competing over French territory. We know that Joan was of high character, brave, active, virtuous, pious, and honest. We know, based on the surviving documents and documents, that Joan possessed special spiritual abilities of prophecy that she claimed were, in fact, the result of direct communications with saints, Angels, and/or spiritual guides.

We know that Joan was born in the small village of Domrémy in the Lorraine region that was located in the heart of a contested area of France that was regularly overrun by English, French, Burgundian, and even mercenary raiding parties who did not claim allegiance to any country. We know that Joan somehow convinced the French King Charles VII of France, by way of a miracle, message, or sign, that Joan was, in fact, the fulfillment of an ancient prophecy that circulated at that time in England and France. This prophecy stated that a Maid, or virgin, from the region of Lorraine would save France and lead her to victory.[8]

> "France will be lost by a woman and saved by a virgin from the oak forests of Lorraine."

---

[8] For several decades, perhaps even centuries, before the arrival of Joan a number of prophecies concerning a young "Maid" who would save France were circulating. The prophecies were attributed to several sources including St. Bede, Euglide of Hungary, and Merlin. Some of these prophecies spoke of a young Maid, or virgin, who would come from the "borders of Lorraine". Joan's home village of Domrémy was near the border of the French Duchies of Bar and Lorraine.

Left: An example of a page taken from the Les Prophecies de Merlin, from Bibliothèque Nationale de France. This manuscript is a French prose text originating in Venice circa 1276, is a composite text, consisting of romance material derived from Galfridian and French Arthurian sources and original political prophecies regarding Italian events of the eleventh, twelfth, and thirteenth centuries. The text is primarily a series of prophecies as related by Merlin to various scribes.

We know from historical accounts that Joan led the French armies to a series of victories over one year from 1429 to 1430AD. We know that Joan of Arc was, in fact, one of the youngest military leaders in history at the age of 17-18 that places her in the same context as Alexander the Great (first battle at the age 16 against a Thracian uprising in his father's absence) and Edward IV of England (led first battles at the ages of 19-20).[9] It was, perhaps, Joan's claims to a divine mission that, above all other aspects, was the most contested element of her painful trial in 1431 where she was questioned repeatedly under harsh conditions regarding the details and nature of her spiritual communications and revelations.

Based on Joan's behavior, words, and deeds, it is reasonable to presume that with she was, as we view things in modern terms, clairvoyant or psychic and that she was able to read into the context of future events before they occurred and see through the outer veils of people, relationships, and events to some degree through an expanded spiritual faculty. This fact was validated by eyewitness testimonies as the fulfillments of her prophetic words came into reality repeatedly. This fact, in alignment with the miraculous nature of her accomplishments, supports

---

[9] Joan was not a simple figurehead as may be envisaged by modern scholars who seek to detracted from her accomplishments. She was routinely on the front lines in battle leading from the front and giving direct orders to officers and soldiers on tactics.

the perspective that she held a mysterious ability that most people have not yet learned to develop within themselves. For example, during the Trial of Rehabilitation that was held through 1452-1456, Father Jean Pasquerel, who knew Joan personally, testified that on May 6, 1429, Jehanne predicted that "tomorrow blood shall flow from my body above my breast." The following day, on May 7, 1429, Joan led an attack and was wounded in the shoulder by an arrow fired from a crossbow.

Although she could neither read nor write, through her efforts Joan brought forth a change in the destiny of three nations of Western Europe and caused the English and Burgundians to be pushed out of France and back into their respective domains. As a result, Joan united France as a nation and altered her destiny. We can reasonably infer, although there is no definitive historical evidence to support the assertion, that through treachery Joan was captured on May 23, 1430, at Compiègne by Burgundian forces after being betrayed by Charles VII and his advisors. She was subsequently sold to the English and kept in confinement and captivity over the course of several months where she was repeatedly mistreated and interrogated.

We know that Joan was eventually convicted on false charges of sorcery and witchcraft by a pro-English ecclesiastical and political tribunal led by a certain Bishop Pierre Cauchon (1371-1442) who was supported by an array of British nobles, Pro-British bishops and legates, and at least one papal representative. We know that Joan was questioned repeatedly and possibly assaulted on at least one occasion while being restrained in chains on a cot in a dingy room while imprisoned in Rouen.[10] Robbed of her privacy and dignity, Joan was perpetually under threat and fatigue exacerbated by food and water deprivation. She was treated as a military prisoner strapped to her bed in chains while being held under constant observation by at least three male English guards who slept in her cell.[11]

We know that Joan was convicted on a variety of allegations that were a part of, at that time, the standard playbook of legal indictments of heresy and treason that were frequently used during the trials of the inquisition.

---

[10] The historical records tell us that the Duke of Warwick, as the leading English representative during Joan's trial who oversaw the education and minority of the English boy-king Henry VI, prevented this from occurring.

[11] Based on the testimony of one witness at the retrial of 1456, even the bed appears to have been removed at some point, so she slept on the floor.

We know that Joan endured and resisted passively for several months without abandoning her dignity. It is obvious from Joan's testimony and behavior that she did her best to navigate through an evolving web of misrepresentation and legal rhetoric, exacerbated by mental gymnastics, that was mercilessly and repeatedly hurled upon her by a group of older and highly educated men. It is clear that Joan maintained her dignity and the integrity of her mission, as communicated by spiritual guides, by not allowing herself to capitulate to the will of manipulative people whom she perceived as threatening the sanctity of her soul, and their own, by trying to induce her to betray the council and advice of her angelic guides whom her inquisitors insisted were false and illusory.

Joan's trial in 1431 was not just a means by which a conviction of Joan could be achieved. Since the tribunal was an English affair, as it were, they could have disposed of Joan whenever they chose. The secular leaders, led by the English, held the real power of the inquiry and they were in a position of absolute authority and could do with Joan as they wished. While some of the members of the tribunal were at odds with one another regarding Joan's legitimacy, the trial was carried out with the highest degree of legal and ecclesiastical precision while, at the same time, willfully disregarding truth and a governance process that would provide a balanced procedure. The inquisitors spent their time trying to induce Joan to betray herself and the promises that she had made to her angelic guides and King Charles VII. Thus, they behaved in a manner that suited their self-interest through a religious-legal, and institutionalized, mechanism. The lines between the two aspects, which are so clearly defined today in Western culture, were blurred.

It is an interesting paradox that the effort to lure and even force Joan to betray herself was the primary goal of Bishop Pierre Cauchon as the lead interrogator and pro-English ecclesiastical legate. While under English influence, he was in charge of the trial but engaged from an ecclesiastical perspective. The realization that certain leading prosecutors sought to find a way to induce Joan by threats into condemning her soul by betraying her spiritual guides makes highly intelligent and educated men such as Bishop Cauchon, and many who supported him, examples of men who were heavily influenced by egotism and self-interest. This is because intelligence is not synonymous with wisdom. The bishop was a highly educated and erudite but he was also under the influence of egotism and corruption that led to spiritual blindness. His fear and egotism led to a mean-spirited disposition. This reality challenges a serious and historical researcher to seek out and perceive a higher purpose regarding the adversarial roles that certain people have played throughout history. Regardless of how objective a student of Joan's wishes to be, a researcher finds that Bishop Cauchon's behavior is characterized by, perhaps, the same egotism of men such as Pontius Pilot and Judas Iscariot. What is vitally important in light of Joan's life and mission, as shall be reviewed in this work, is to understand the influences of the age in which Joan lived.

This perspective is supported by several first-hand accounts of the bishop's fervent dedication to his active and callous targeting and antagonism as one who, as was testified at the Trial of Nullification in 1452-1456, took a harsh and maligned approach towards Joan in a personal way.[12] The bishop had the option to treat Joan either as a secular or ecclesiastical prisoner. At that time, leaving Joan in the hands of the English was a far worse destiny than ecclesiastical prison, and Bishop Cauchon ensured that Joan was held as a hostile secular prisoner. Many of those present were deeply divided and did not approve of the bishop's approach to the trial, yet his absolute authority was undeniable especially when Rouen and the castle were filled with English troops.[13] Here, we see an example of the bishop's true disposition despite all of the formality and attempts to present the trial as legitimate, legal, and objective:

> "...on the day when the bishop and several others declared her a heretic, relapsed, and returned to her evil deeds, because, in prison, she had resumed a man's dress, the bishop, coming out of the prison, met the Earl of Warwick and a great many English with him, to whom he said, laughing, in a loud and clear voice: "Farewell! farewell! it is done; be of good cheer," or such-like words..."[14]

Thus, we see the leading prosecutor and mediator of the trial of 1431 rejoice because he had a legal precedent for executing someone who wore women's clothing. In modern times, especially in the West, this is absurd,

---

[12] I shall use the term "Trial of Nullification" as synonymous with "Trial of Rehabilitation" and "Retrial" throughout this work. These terms are synonymous.

[13] Joan was held in Rouen at the Castle of Philip Augustus.

[14] The Retrial of 1456. The English translation of the trial files from 1902. From the book: Jeanne d'Arc Maid of Orléans Deliverer of France. Edited by T. Douglas Murray, Deposition of Brother Martin Ladvenu of the Order of Saint Dominic, and of the Convent of Saint Jacques at Rouen.

and using that technicality came across as absurd to many of the 15th century as well. In addition, accounts support the fact that there was a deliberate effort to falsify court transcripts during the trial as was testified at the Trial of Nullification:

> "On writing the said Process, I was often opposed by my Lord of Beauvais (Bishop Cauchon) and the Masters, who wanted to compel me to write according to their fancy, and against what I had myself heard. And when there was something which did not please them, they forbade it to be written, saying that it did not serve the Process; but I nevertheless wrote only according to my hearing and knowledge."[15]

Despite Joan's best efforts to protect her integrity as an individual and her spiritual mission, in light of the allegations that were clearly politically motivated, she had an opportunity to recant during a legal event known as the "Abjuration". Joan confessed that, as it was explained to her, she did not know what that legal term truly meant. This is not surprising given the manipulative way in which the court representatives behaved. The English, evidently, had promised to allow Joan to take Mass and move to an ecclesiastical prison in exchange for removing her men's clothing. Joan claims that they did not honor this promise. Additionally, Joan had no formal legal representation as the man appointed to her was a pro-English legate, so she was truly on her own. She recanted after seeing that she had been fed misinformation by her appointed legal representative. Joan was burned at the stake on May 30, 1431, at the age of 19.

Much later, in 1452 at the request of Joan's mother, King Charles VII instigated a retrial known today as the "Trial of Rehabilitation" or "Trial of Nullification" and was authorized by Pope Callixtus III. The Pope, through his delegates, formed a tribunal that consisted of 124 judges and 22 witnesses who knew Joan and provided testimony. The retrial concluded in 1456. As to be expected, the retrial pronounced Joan innocent and declared her a martyr. Therefore, in political terms, Joan was convicted and sentenced to die by a pro-English political tribunal (with Papal consent) and later redeemed by a pro-French political tribunal (again with Papal consent).

---

[15] Ibid. Deposition of Maitre Guillaume Manchon, Canon of the Collegiate Church of Notre Dame d'Audely, etc.

Regardless of the inherent flaws of political decision-making, which almost always exist in the sphere of public affairs, Joan's spiritual mission was accomplished and she was, in fact, later recognized as a genuine heroine of France and Catholic martyr. 100 years later, Joan became a public symbol of the Catholic League. In 1803, she was declared a national symbol of France by Napoleon Bonaparte. Joan was officially canonized by the Catholic Church in 1920. Today, Joan of Arc is recognized as one of the nine patron saints of France.[16] Since her martyrdom, Joan has gained the admiration and appreciation of individuals, theologians, military leaders, politicians, and historians across the world. As an individual who was deeply in touch with the powers of destiny as an active principle in the events of history that he often referred to in his speeches and writings, Winston Churchill describes Joan of Arc as:

"...an Angel of Deliverance, the noblest patriot of France, the most splendid of her heroes, the most beloved of her saints, the most inspiring of all her memories, the peasant Maid, the ever-shining, ever-glorious Joan of Arc. In the poor, remote hamlet of Domrémy, on the fringe of the Vosges Forest, she served at the inn. She rode the horses of travelers, bareback, to water. She wandered on Sundays into the woods, where there were shrines, and a legend that some day from these oaks would arise one to save France.

"In the fields where she tended her sheep the saints of God, who grieved for France, rose before her in visions. St. Michael himself appointed her, by right divine, to command the armies of liberation. Joan shrank at first from the awful duty, but when he returned attended by St. Margaret and St. Catherine, patronesses of the village church, she obeyed their command. There welled in the heart of the Maid a pity for the realm of France, sublime, perhaps miraculous, certainly invincible."[17]

So, a simple farmgirl emerged from obscurity and led the French armies to victory during the apex of the Hundred Years' War and died a martyr's death. This, from a traditional and dogmatic view, should not have been

---

[16]The nine patron saints of France are the Virgin Mary and Holy Mother, the Archangel Michael, Bishop Denis of Paris, Martin of Tours, Louis IX "The Saint", Joan of Arc, Remigius Bishop of Reims, Thérèse de Lisieux. Petronilla, and Radegund.

[17] Churchill, Winston. A History of the English-Speaking Peoples, Vol. 1, The Birth of Britain (London: Cassell, 1956), p. 417.

feasible. As shall be discussed, this was only able to occur because higher spiritual beings including the Christ were working directly through Joan at the moment in time. Her successes were not the result of Joan's egotism. This divine influence and direction occurred by way of the council of her spiritual guardians with whom she communicated through a genuine and expanded perception that came through to her consciousness as voices (i.e., to hear clearly or "clairaudience"), visions (i.e., to see clearly "clairvoyance"), and feelings (i.e., to feel clearly or "clairsentience").[18]

Through the influences of her angelic guides, and her painful martyrdom, Joan posthumously rose to the level of a national hero and a patron saint of France. The liberation of France, and the introduction of the forces behind it, was accomplished over the course of one year between 1429 and 1430. The recognition of Joan's contributions on a global level, however, did not occur publicly until centuries after her death and even today the significance of her contribution is not yet realized. Hopefully, through the lectures and insights of Dr. Rudolf Steiner (1861-1925), this study will enable a more comprehensive view of Joan's mission so that people can begin to appreciate Joan and her accomplishments in a more expanded and factual way that considers the true nature of why Joan was born, the circumstances of her life, and why it was important to world history.

As is the case with genuine martyrs who, having received an authentic spiritual summons to embark on a mission for a higher cause, Joan was essentially alone during the final months of her life with the exception, of course, of the presence of her spiritual guides and her hostile captors. Despite the oppressive presence of the English prison guards who slept in her cell, she had no visitors, family, or friends to converse with or confide to. One can imagine Joan, as a captured eagle imprisoned in a cage, lying helplessly on a cot in a dingy prison cell for months on end with no privacy restrained in iron shackles and chains living in a perpetual state of testing, stress, degradation, hope, and apprehension. However, her confidence never appeared to waiver based on historical accounts.

During this period, Joan's moments of peace were separated only by subsequent rounds of hostile legal questions, jibes, insults, threats, and

---

[18] These are modern terms that describe aspects of psychic ability, as spiritual experience does, in fact, take on different forms based on the disposition of the person.

even assaults by her captors.[19] It was not a fitting end to someone of Joan's high mind and caliber yet, in the spirit of genuine spiritual martyrs, she passed through the membrane of death with her spirit intact. She passed through the window of death chained to a wooden stake in utter agony having preserved the integrity of her mission and her soul. She remained loyal to the directives given to her by the Christ, Archangel Michael, and His divine messengers regardless of the severity of Joan's personal trials.

When contemplating Joan's life, it is appropriate to consider the historical fact that women of the 15th century, especially uneducated farm women, were considered a commodity and were lowly regarded. Women possessed no legal rights and very few social freedoms. Many were simply married off to family friends, acquaintances, or in the noble sphere were used as political pawns. Women of that period were regularly abused and taken for granted. Arranged marriages were common and often occurred at an early age, thus women typically had no choice in their spouses. It seems evident that Joan was well-treated by her family and lived a healthy youth with a close family. Her father appears to have been an overly protective man in the best sense. Given the conditions of the times, a caring father would certainly keep a close eye on his daughter if he truly cared about her. In social terms, Joan broke through barriers, and thus she could be viewed today as a pioneer and early leader of women's rights. That was not, however, Joan's task. Her task, as she relayed on several occasions including the French inquiry at Poitiers in 1429 was:

1. "...that she was sent from the God of Heaven in favor of the noble Dauphin, to replace him in his kingdom,
2. to raise the siege of Orléans, and
3. to conduct the King to Rheims for his consecration; and that first she must write to the English and command them to retire, for such was the Will of God."[20]

The reality of Joan's accomplishments in light of the social, political, and economic barriers of the period makes the accomplishments of her life all

---

[19] Joan claims that an attempt at an assault did occur, but the records do not reveal any further details. It appears from records that the attempt was prevented by the Duke of Warwick.

[20] The English translation of the trial files from 1902. From the book: Jeanne d'Arc Maid of Orléans Deliverer of France. Edited by T. Douglas Murray, Deposition of Maître François Garivel Councillor-General to the King.

the more unique and impressive given the fact that she was accepted as a leader of the French peoples and the future King Charles VII during a medieval period of poverty, war, disease, and famine. This is not an easy thing to accomplish in any time period. Despite her seemingly outlandish claims to divine messages, Joan impressed and was befriended by many of the French nobles, captains, and soldiers that she came in contact with. She influenced several English and Burgundian nobles as well who acknowledged her abilities as a seer and potential healer. Through her chastity, bravery, and dedication to her spiritual principles and the mission as bequeathed unto her by her spiritual guides, she influenced and changed the lives of many people.

As history teaches us, there are always political motives for any kind of public affirmation of someone as a national saint, hero, or martyr but in the case of Joan, each of these perspectives is valid. Regardless of one's perspective on what the requirements are to be a genuine saint, there is a general sense and acceptance that something very special and unique happened with Joan. The truth is that the lives of people such as Joan do not occur frequently...at least in public terms. As is the case with each individual in the world, the lives and missions of individuals such as Joan who led a world-historic destiny are never the result of coincidence.

Rather, the lives that these people lead are always the result of activity, will, planning, destiny, and fulfillment. This reality is the outcome of a process that is at work in human history that is overseen by divine spiritual guides and guardians. Some people, such as Joan, served and will serve in the future a broader purpose for the benefit of humanity while others act as roadblocks who throw the rightful progress of human evolution off-track. These facts are often felt and sensed by those who approach the lives of individuals of world-historic significance. Genuine spiritual research always confirms the reality that a fulfillment, or step to a future fulfillment, of some kind, was, and is, at work in the lives of people throughout the world. Sometimes these fulfillments affect large numbers of people.

By the time of Joan's public activity that began in 1429, France had been effectively divided into three separate spheres of political and economic autonomy. The political entities were competing with each other for dominance. In actuality, the English invasion of France began not with King Henry V at the Battle of Agincourt on October 25, 1415, when he achieved a significant military victory over the French despite being vastly outnumbered,[21] but rather with the Battle of Crécy on August 26, 1346, led by King Edward III. Like Agincourt, it was a turning point for England despite facing an enemy force of superior numbers. As a descendent of the Lancastrian house that had usurped the royal line of the Edwards during the uprising of Henry Bolingbroke against Richard II, this rivalry eventually led to a Civil War in England known today as the Wars of the Roses.[22]

The unlikely victory at Agincourt brought France to her knees and led to a crisis point as the English and Burgundians pushed further into France. Both nations acquired land and villages and split up territory while raiding the French countryside looting, burning, and committing crimes against French villages and commoners at will. The English became known to the French peasantry as "black knights". Raiding parties stole cattle, looted and burned homes, assaulted and kidnapped women, and generally wreaked havoc across the countryside. Rebuilding homes and property after a raid was common and poverty and fear was an integrated element of French life. Starving French families and refugees were frequently seen moving through the landscape as they were driven from their homes as the battle for domination raged between opposing forces. Desperate circumstances turned brother against brother in many villages and towns of France. After 1415, France began to crumble.

Joan of Arc's name, in modern times, compels a discerning listener to stop and ponder what exactly occurred during her lifetime because on the surface a piece of the riddle is clearly missing. To some, it is simple nonsense. For others, it is a sign that God, and the Angels, work directly through human beings. In the misogynistic culture of 15th century England and France, a poor and uneducated farm woman of that day and age could not have possibly have led a medieval army to victory out of mere egotism or the power of personality alone. Even the idea of using the myth of the Maid of Lorraine to inspire the people by those in authority, such as Charles VI and VII, would not have convinced anyone or inspired the French

---

[21] These two competing factions of the English royal house, in the Henrys of the red rose and the Edwards of the white rose, would result in what is known today the "Wars of the Roses" that began shortly after the death of Joan of Arc with a feud between the "Yorkists" who rallied under Richard 3rd Duke of York and those loyal to Henry VI who descended from the "Lancastrian" line. As the forces of Joan forced the English out of France, so those forces turned against each other in England and nearly brought the country to ruination.

[22] This event eventually led to a civil war in England now referred to as the Wars of the Roses between the Lancastrians (Red Rose) and the Yorkists (White Rose).

army without a genuine aspect to her individuality. Joan gladly provided that evidence.

Joan's special significance is further revealed in overcoming the various challenges on her path that were colored by confirmed prophecies, miracles, and seemingly miraculous victories. An example of this emerges when, as proof of her identity, Joan successfully identified the future King of France Charles the VII at his court in Chinon despite his efforts to conceal his identity and deceive her. Joan later revealed that she was led to a successful identification of Charles VII by her spiritual guides. She never, however, publicly revealed the substance of the sign that she presented to Charles. It is clear, however, that this sign convinced Charles that she was in fact, a person of special ability and that he should follow her advice to attack the English at the Siege of Orléans.

This effort to convince Charles of her identity and task was successful only due to Joan's expanded powers of clairvoyance, and the direction of her spiritual guardians, when she correctly identified him in a crowd having never seen him before. This was followed by a private meeting that lasted several hours. After proof was achieved, Joan's challenging and chaotic journey was characterized by barriers, roadblocks, and the task to overcome a form of lethargy that had overwhelmed the French people and was exacerbated by a perpetually vacillating King Charles VII. This was the result of years of war, defeatism, and poor decision-making by Charles VII that had corrupted the people of France into a form of fatalism and hopelessness.

Of the several aspects regarding Joan's life that Dr. Steiner chose to reveal, he confirms that Joan's task and martyrdom extended beyond France into England and Western Europe. This, in turn, impacted the world. Her accomplishment has subsequently resonated into the future as to the fulfillment of the destiny of the nations in the world, including America, whether we are aware of it or not. As shall be demonstrated, given Steiner's insights, each country in the West and the world is somehow imbued with the spiritual substance brought to the world by the Christ, the Archangel Michael, and the spiritual hierarchies that now resides within the human being thanks to Joan's victory.

It is important to note, however, that during this struggle many people on either side of the battle lines, as driven by their individual destinies and dispositions, played a variety of roles based on their unique soul-histories and fulfillments. Regardless of their role or relationship to Joan, virtually all were transformed in some way. Therefore, it is not appropriate to assume that all of the English or Burgundians were against Joan any more than it is to say that all the French were vehemently supporting her. The betrayal of Joan by the ever-changeable and weak-willed King Charles VII who was vehemently supported by Joan and endorsed him as the destined leader of the French peoples during that moment in history is a clear indication of that reality.

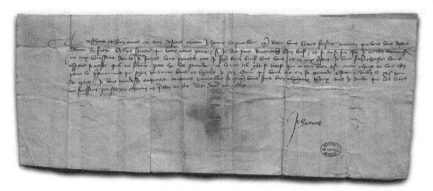

Above: A surviving letter from Joan written during her stay at Sully Castle to the inhabitants of Reims. Dated to March 16, 1430. This letter would have been dictated by Joan to a page, or herald, and then signed directly by Jeanne. There are nine surviving letters, either as medieval copies or originals, signed by Joan that are known to exist.[23]

---

[23] "To my very dear and good friends, men of the Church, bourgeois, and other inhabitants of the town of Reims Very dear and well-beloved, whom I greatly desire to see: I Jeanne the Virgin have received your letters mentioning that you fear facing a siege. Know then that you will not, if I can meet them soon. And if it should so happen that I do not intercept them and they come against you, then shut your gates, for I will be with you shortly. And if they are there, I will make them put on their spurs in such haste that they won't be able to do so; and their time will be short, for this will be soon. I won't write you anything else for the present, except that you should always be obedient and loyal. I pray to God to hold you in His keeping. Written at Sully the 16th day of March. I would send you some further news which would make you quite happy, but I fear that the letters would be captured on the road, and that the news would be seen." Signed: Jehanne.

Left: Joan was taught to write her signature while on campaign probably in 1429. This image is a surviving original signature from a letter that she dictated. It appears from the script that Joan signed this slowly and carefully.

As a result, as is the case with any civil war or conflict where multiple streams of influences and interests come together, we should view the personalities involved in her life in terms of their constraints and dispositions and not assume that the groups of people involved in that tumultuous period felt, acted, and behaved in a consistent manner. Many of the English and Burgundians, for example, considered themselves genuine Christian knights and were not interested in endorsing the execution of a poor farm woman who was clearly leading a peculiar, important, and unique destiny. Others were driven by their lower impulses. Anyone who possessed some measure of discernment, however, including her most vehement enemies could see that she was unique and that something out of the ordinary was occurring. Some (or so they later claimed) tried to avoid being involved with the trial but under threat of death were compelled to take part.

> "I gave no opinion during the Trial, but allowed myself to affix my signature, under compulsion from the Bishop of Beauvais. I made excuses to him...finally, the Bishop forced me to subscribe as others had done, saying that otherwise some ill would befall me for having come to Rouen. I say, too, that threats were also used against Maître Jean Lohier and Maître Nicolas de Houppeville, who, not wishing to take part in the Trial, were threatened with the penalty of drowning."[24]

Some of Joan's opponents, such as John of Lancaster, Duke of Bedford, and Bishop Cauchon, were maddened by Joan's gifts and her stubborn resiliency. As a result, they were driven to a path of antagonism and violence. Everyone, however, including those who supported Joan to the end, behaved in something of a conflicted way. In light of these facts, it

---

[24] The English translation of the trial files from 1902. From the book: <u>Jeanne d'Arc Maid of Orléans Deliverer of France</u>. Edited by T. Douglas Murray, Deposition of Maître Guillaume Delachambre Master in Arts and Medicine who participated as a legate in the Trial of 1431.

makes the path that Joan chose, the definitive path by which was clearly and definitively brought to her waking consciousness by her spiritual guides, even more endearing to those who can perceive some of the elements of the true nature of her task that led, per the path of her destiny and a higher cause that is not visible on the surface, to her painful and necessary martyrdom.[25]

Many people who sense a connection to those times and events will inevitably feel an inner pull to that chaotic period in French and English history and Joan's life. As is the way of things, one is inevitably inclined to antagonism or sympathy. Through the limited view of hindsight, one feels as though something important happened at that moment of history behind the scenes, as it were, somehow. However, the mystery behind the veil of perception is just out of reach and as a result, never comes into focus. Now, thanks to the gifts given to us by Rudolf Steiner who provided publicly certain details regarding Joan's life as only a genuine spiritual initiate could, a researcher can take another step forward and gain a better view of what truly happened during that chaotic and troubling time in human history. We can allow ourselves to recognize and be influenced by her martyrdom as we move into the future and look back into the past in light of a true and genuine spiritual science, and thus gain a clearer view of how she impacted countless people and was vital to the destiny of the rightful and appropriate forward progress of the world. [26]

Before this can occur, however, a proper study of Joan's mission and life must be observed in light of certain foundational spiritual principles, facts, and relationships that are only revealed through spiritual science as have been brought forth publicly by Dr. Rudolf Steiner. Joan's task was not about

---

[25] Joan's faculty of prophecy was based on a genuine form of clairvoyance, the nature of which shall be described in this work as revealed by Dr. Steiner. Through her clairvoyance she received detailed messages, and had discussions, with spiritual guides. On her way to Chinon to visit the future Charles VII, she said "I shall last a year, and but little longer: we must think to do good work in that year" and later "I am not afraid... I was born to do this". These comments, which recur repeatedly throughout her life as she carried out her mission, reveal someone who perceived the beginning, the challenges of the task and the middle, and the ending which, based on her comments, clearly indicate someone who understood that her martyrdom would be necessary. In the spirit of the Christ, Joan carried out her mission for the sole benefit of humanity knowing, and accepting, that the ending of her life was going to be, in fact, a beginning and was a necessary aspect of her destiny...

[26] I point out that the contributions of the Rudolf Steiner Archives have greatly enabled a work such as this to be completed. Without them, this work could not have been completed. Refer to www.rsarchive.org.

being "Joan" in an egoistic sense. Hers was not a life that was led in the vein of the Roman Caesars or Napoleon who sought self-aggrandizement, wealth, power, and played historic roles in the process. No, Joan's life was quite different. Her task comes in light of the circumstances of human evolution that occurred in the 15th century. This circumstance can only be rightly considered in light of a perpetual battle that occurs between the forces of light and darkness who, unbeknownst to the masses, work for or against the appropriate transformation of humanity.

The circumstances of the 15th century that required Joan's intervention were direct outcomes of the activities of the guiding leaders of humanity who were confronting and overcoming the effects wrought by the opposing powers upon humanity. The opposing forces had to be confronted and dealt with in a certain way. The soul of Joan, who supported this task, was uniquely suited for that mission in spiritual terms. Steiner reveals that the outcome that Joan achieved cannot be accomplished in the same way today given the conditions of the age in which we live. He tells us that Joan was a vehicle who worked directly on behalf of the Christ and the Archangel Michael. She played a critical role in a global crisis that had become concentrated in the French, English, and Burgundian nations. The battleground for the future of Europe, and the world, was at stake and was concentrated within the relatively small geographic area of France.

As mentioned previously, and shall be reaffirmed throughout this work, it is only through someone like Dr. Steiner, as a genuine spiritual initiate, that a sincere researcher can begin to grasp in a meaningful way how the movements and activities of higher beings who influence and guide humanity led to an intercession where they worked directly through Joan to accomplish a certain goal. This type of study is necessarily imperfect and one that, hopefully, will encourage further research on the spiritual turning point of the 15th century. It is my hope that this work will garner some attention as to the true nature of Joan's life and her mission as she was, in fact, a genuine martyr and heroine who gave her life for a higher cause. During the course of a study of this kind, there are always new truths to be discovered...

This study will not address all of the dimensions of Joan's life and mission, but perhaps it will bring to the forefront those facts and details that Steiner brought to us that has, for some time, been largely passed over in the public mind and yet are openly available to anyone who seeks them out. Before one can appreciate the true nature of Joan's accomplishments, however, it is appropriate for any reader to consider a high-level overview of some foundational spiritual facts, as brought to us by Dr. Steiner, and thus embrace a broader perspective of Joan's task.

Chapter 1: A Foundation in Light of Spiritual Science

In light of the hidden aspects of Joan's life and to grasp the importance and significance of her accomplishments as inspired and driven by the great spiritual leaders of humanity, it is necessary to provide something of a brief, if inadequate, overview and foundation upon which those who are not familiar with some of the foundational aspects of spiritual science as revealed by Dr. Rudolf Steiner can take a step closer. It is only through these insights that researchers can achieve a more robust perspective on Joan's birth, mission, life, and death.[27]

The study of the genuine spiritual truths in life, the cosmos, and human history is a lifelong study and practicum of spiritual transformation for each individual who embarks on the seeker's path. It is not a dogmatic study that refrains from expanding outside of the box, as it were. All people struggle with addressing and challenging false dogmas that we have inherited in our personal experiences, cultures, and/or educations. Most of the time, if spiritual studies are undertaken, they tend to be focused on a kind of philosophic materialism or are analyses that provide little or no insights or depth. A true study of history and the human being considers the true nature of the spiritual worlds and how they relate to humanity and the physical world. This pursuit, therefore, seeks to build a bridge. The great minds of history have always sought this knowledge including people such as Thomas Aquinas, Heraclitus, Plato, Aristotle, and Pythagoras. In the ancient world, these people were a part of a task to bring the otherwise hidden knowledge of the universe to humanity by way of what was formerly referred to as "the mysteries". In modern times, this term has faded into the past and is no longer used.

Sound knowledge comes for those who seek to build and maintain a mature bridge to the spiritual worlds. Casual and immature activity in this field is dangerous and often leads to false observations, and attitudes, that

---

[27] All human beings are born into a state of amnesia when we come into the world. We are all constrained by limitations, cultures, attitudes, aptitudes, etc. However, genuine knowledge of the spiritual worlds has been brought forth by authentic teachers in a genuine, valid, and truthful way regardless of culture. Therefore, we can turn to them to guide us forward. Many people claim to bring genuine spiritual insights, and some do, but much of what is written is based on superstitions or false observations. Thus, many superstitions abound in modern times and as a result, people simply turn away. Thus, we turn to a genuine spiritual initiate, such as Dr. Steiner, who came to humanity with a mission to reveal the truth of the spiritual worlds and how they relate to humanity.

must later be corrected and purged. In modern times, our knowledge of the spiritual worlds is also enhanced by the testimony of those who have traveled beyond the barrier that separates this world from the next through genuine spiritual perception and near-death experiences. In the latter, the testimony provided is truly empirical in the sense that those who have crossed the bridge return tell us about their journeys in an objective way. Thus, knowledge comes from a variety of sources and we most always retain an open mind. Grasping certain basic spiritual facts, as reflected here, hopefully, will enable one to prepare to lay a sound foundation that can come to fruition and maturity through a genuine spiritual initiate and teacher.

This foundation is based on the published research, lectures, and books of Dr. Rudolf Steiner, as a modern genuine spiritual initiate. I organized this chapter so that it reviews six fundamental aspects as revealed by the great leaders, and initiates, of humanity. The six aspects that I have outlined here are not firm or rigid esoteric guidelines, but rather are intended to assist a new researcher towards a more robust study of Joan's mission and task in light of this particular work. This chapter is not comprehensive and, as always, one should consult the sources of information provided by way of the references provided here for further research. This chapter was produced by way of Dr. Steiner's body of knowledge that are objective observations of spiritual facts that he shared publicly.

Dr. Steiner conducted many lectures and published books that outline a valid spiritual path suitable for the conditions of the modern age that will enable a seeker to develop and attain spiritual transformation. It is those works that should be consulted for the proper path and foundation. For those who are already well-versed in valid esoteric and spiritual principles, this overview will be redundant but for those to whom these principles have not been renewed in their consciousness or it is the first time they have considered them in a spiritual-historical study, it is a decent if imperfect foundation upon which understanding Joan's life and mission can be grasped.[28]

---

[28] Refer to Rudolf Steiner's Occult Science, An Outline, How to Know Higher Worlds: A Modern Path of Initiation, Knowledge of The Higher Worlds and Its Attainment: On Consciousness, Dream Life and Initiation, and his body of knowledge, much of which can be found on www.rsarchive.org. The works of Edgar Cayce are also helpful to begin to an esoteric study of spiritual ideas, principles, and realities.

Key aspects of spiritual studies, much of which has been suppressed by church dogma and secular materialism over the centuries, include foundational elements such as reincarnation and karma, humanity's spiritual history, and our relationship to the Angels and the Spiritual Hierarchies including the Christ, the Archangel Michael, and the opposing powers. The aspects outlined here are not comprehensive nor should they take precedence over any of Steiner's, or a genuine spiritual initiate, teachings, or research. Any disparities are the sole responsibility of the author and are not intentional. There are volumes of considerations and details behind these basic foundational aspects that require time, commitment, and study...

Aspect 1: The Spiritual Hierarchies & the Guardians of Humanity[29]

"...certain events in the more ancient history of mankind can be rightly understood only when we not merely observe the forces and faculties of the personalities themselves, but when we realize at the outset that through the personalities in question, as through instruments, Beings are working who allow their deeds to stream down from higher worlds into our world. We must realize that these Beings cannot take direct hold of the physical facts of our existence because, on account of the present stage of their development, they cannot incarnate in a physical body which draws its constituents from the physical world.

"If, therefore, they desire to work within our physical world, they must make use of the physical human being — of his deeds, but also of his intellect, his powers of understanding. We find the influence and penetration of such Beings of the higher world the more clearly in evidence the farther back we go in the ages of the evolution of humanity. But it must not be imagined that this downpouring of forces and activities from the higher worlds into the physical world through human beings has ever ceased; it continues even into our own time."[30]

Within the ongoing struggle of humanity's transformation, as each individual strives in our daily lives from birth through maturity and to death, regardless of one's awareness thereabouts, each one of us is guided by higher beings who stand above physical existence and do not incarnate in the physical world. These lofty spiritual beings oversee the world and humanity over the course of long cycles of time, form, movement, and transformation. They influence and oversee the varied aspects of human activity including form, destiny, cultures, and nations. Humanity was born, progresses, and changes over time. Humanity is not fully developed and we still have a long way to go with many challenges and bridges to cross. There is an overarching process at work that requires vast cycles of time to complete. The higher beings who govern the various spheres of spiritual

---

[29] Rudolf Steiner provides many insights regarding the spiritual hierarchies and the relationships of the divine higher beings to each other and humanity. Refer to Steiner's Occult Science - An Outline (Book), The Mission of Individual Folk Souls (Lecture), Cosmic Memory (Lecture), and The Mission of Folk-Souls (Lecture) for further research.
[30] Steiner, Rudolf. Occult History Lecture 2, Stuttgart, 28th December 1910.

activity work collaboratively based on regular cycles and cadences under the guidance and leadership of a vast hierarchy.

The higher and lofty beings who oversee humanity exist within varying relationships to one another and humanity and each brings a unique influence to the world based on their task and the conditions and needs of the world and humanity at any given moment in time. This is further characterized by the limitations, goals, and configuration of the human being. Dr. Steiner reveals that divine beings cannot incarnate in physical forms at the present moment; thus, they work through human beings in a variety of hidden ways. They work within the human being and through divine messengers.

Rudolf Steiner reveals, as have many genuine philosophers and spiritual seekers and initiates throughout history, that the activities of humanity and the world are overseen and influenced by a vast hierarchy of spiritual beings who exist in a structure of nine grades or dimensions of activity. Over the entire breadth of history, cycles of continuing changes are brought to humanity deliberately out of the spiritual worlds per the will and plan of divine beings. Higher beings work to bring forth changes through activities, impulses, and influences based on the conditions of the age in which humanity exists at any particular moment. The modern secular views of evolution and nature as isolated forces that seem to work on their own are meaningless without considering the activities of the beings who work out of the spiritual worlds and how their thoughts and activities interpolate the physical plane. The human being and the physical world are a reflection and manifestation of the spiritual worlds. Humanity is a microcosm that was born out of the spiritual worlds, and the will of higher beings, that reflects the construct of the cosmos, or macrocosm.

Serving the divine higher beings are many messengers, workers, and representatives. They come in many forms and work through all of the cultures across the world. In relation to the whole, this is a much smaller group of people that consists of mature and highly developed human beings who incarnate in the physical world and bring spiritual impulses through tasks and missions per the will and directive of higher beings. These messengers and individuals are the bridges between the divine and the physical world. Thus, as higher beings do not incarnate in physical form, they necessarily work through people who are well-prepared and sufficiently mature to carry out the will of divine beings.

The one exception of a higher being who incarnated in the physical world, having never done so before, is the Sun-God, the Christ, who incarnated in the body of Jesus in 30AD and walked the earth for three years with the task of redeeming humanity and bringing the path and the impulse of light, freedom, and transformation to the world. His entry into the physical world is the central aspect, and turning point, of human evolution. His divine impulse, which inspires all human beings to true spiritual freedom and transformation, continues to unfold in the world and humanity and shall do so until the end of the world. The Christ walked the earth and performed His mission on behalf of humanity precisely at the midpoint of human history. As His forces continue to permeate the world over time, human beings transform as they become more influenced, or imbued, by His forces and being. Some people have carried His impulse directly within them, as a living spiritual being, in order to serve a broader purpose.

The nine grades of higher beings work through seven spiritual-planetary spheres of activity, each of which is associated with a physical planetary body in our solar system. There are, in fact, seven spiritual spheres, cities, planes that correlate to the planets in our solar system and not nine as modern astronomers have agreed upon in modern times. Thus, there is a difference many times between how the physical sciences in the modern world perceive something that is a physical manifestation of a spiritual being, or sphere of activity, and the actual spiritual fact behind it. The higher beings are not, in a materialistic sense, inhabiting a physical planet nor are they confined by these planes of activity in a physical way. The exalted higher beings of the Spiritual Hierarchies work in alignment with their spheres and planes of activity.[31]

The higher beings possess unique attributes and relationships to one another and humanity. As Steiner reveals, the relationships and activities of these beings are complex and evolve over time. The divine beings that are closest to humanity are referred to as Angels, or Angeloi, by Rudolf Steiner, the spiritual initiates and teachers, and descriptions that have survived into the modern age.[32] Our guardian angels, who exist one stage above humanity, act as guides and messengers who carry out the will of the Archangels. They oversee each individual's transformation from one life to

---

[31] Key cadences, for example, can be seen in the numbers 7 and 12.

[32] For example, refer to On the Celestial and Ecclesiastical Hierarchies by Pseudo-Dionysius the Areopagite who lived in the 5th century AD.

the next in alignment with specific rules of engagement and a plan of growth and development.

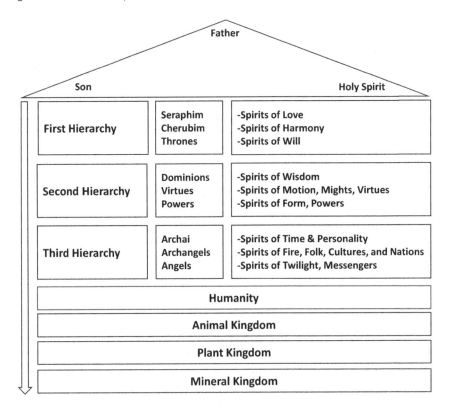

The stage above the angelic sphere is the plane of the Archangels. The will of the Archangels is passed onto humanity through the angelic grade of higher beings. Each plane, or grade, of activity in the hierarchy, is intimately linked to the one below and above it. As Steiner reveals, the hierarchy of celestial divine beings exists within three larger groups of activity.[33]

A deeper understanding of the unique and important nature of Joan's mission, the substance of which truly remains a mystery at the heart of it, is only possible when considering the roles of what Rudolf Steiner refers to as Folk Spirits in the destiny of cultures and nations. These guiding beings belong to the divine plane, as it were, of the Archangels. The Archangels, or Folk Spirits, are two stages above humanity where, as one of their primary

---

[33] Refer to Steiner, Rudolf. The Spiritual Hierarchies, Their Reflection in the Physical World. April, 1909. GA110 for more information.

tasks, they guide the evolution of human beings through the development and transformation of nations and cultures.

> "In order that, distributed amongst the various peoples of the Earth, the progressive development of successive epochs may be realized, in order that the widely differing ethnic types may be molded by a particular geographical area or community of language, in order that a particular form — language, architecture, art or science may flourish and their various metamorphoses receive all that the Spirit of the Age can pour into mankind — for this we need the Folk Spirits, who, in the hierarchy of higher Beings, belong to the Archangels."[34]

Thus, the mission of the Folk Souls is to work through nations and cultures as an integrated part of humanity's progress. Each nation is destined to transform over time. There is movement within the Spiritual Hierarchies as some of the higher beings are at different stages within their ranks. Like all beings, they too progress to the next stage of the hierarchy having completed their tasks and delivered impulses to humanity in accordance with their individual missions.

The leading Archangels act as regents and govern in cycles of 300-400 years each bringing a certain influence to humanity. Thus, they possess a quality of acting as regents who bring their impulses to humanity through successive increments of time, which is a characteristic of the Archai, who exist one stage higher. The Archangel Michael, as the leading member of the seven Archangels, has his seat in the Sun Sphere that is the highest of the seven planetary spiritual spheres of activity and, like all of the Archangels and higher beings of a divine nature, works in alignment with the revelation of the Christ impulse and the light that He brings to humanity and the world. The current regency cycle began in 1879 and is under the leadership of the Archangel Michael.[35]

> "...the spirits we count to the hierarchy of the Archangels rule only for three to four centuries. They alternate in such a way that about six or seven come one after the other, while a spirit of the ages is ruling. So that we have that archangel we call Oriphiel in the time of

---

[34] Steiner, Rudolf. The Mission of the Individual Folk-Souls, Lecture 1, "Angels, Folk Spirits, Time Spirits: their part in the Evolution of Mankind."

[35] "El" in Hebrew means of "of God". In esoteric science, it also means "the goal" or the "the way". Refer to Steiner, Rudolf, The Gospel of John, Third Lecture, March 5, 1906.

the Mystery of Golgotha. Then Anael, Zachariel, Raphael, Samael, Gabriel rule successively; and now since 1879 we have the government of that archangel we call Michael. So, we have, if we look at the spiritual worlds, the higher government of the spirits of the ages and subordinate to them, the successive governments of Archangels."[36]

We should not confuse the leading Archangel Michael with the other Folk Spirits who also belong to the realm of the Archangels. Michael brings a certain impulse within the overall family of nations and thus influences humanity as a global impulse. Yet, Michael also works within certain cultures and nations with greater intensity as required for a given age as heralds, as it were, and bearers of Christ's' task at a given moment in time. In other words, Michael engages with humanity in anticipation of a future fulfillment as required outside of his designated cycle. As revealed by Steiner, Michael was working through Joan of Arc in anticipation of his approaching regency cycle.

Thus, cultural impulses that are brought to humanity are embedded within a framework, or family, of nations. As a cultural impulse is introduced and it reaches its apex, the world moves forward thus leaving countries and nations in place which, in turn, fall into a steady-state or a state of decline as they take their place amongst the world of nations. For example, the Greek culture bought forth a certain quality for humanity that fell into decline and was absorbed into the Roman cultural impulse that carried it forward in a transformed way, and thus it spread out amongst humanity. Steiner reveals that there are some seven periods, or epochs, of spiritual-cultural impulses that humanity is passing through.

During these changes, aspects may fall away and are resurrected in a new form later on. Many nations and cultures remain, transform, and sometimes split off or are absorbed into other cultures as the forward progress of humanity's evolution continues. These changes always work in accordance with the divine plan. Activity and change never cease. The construct of the world changes and takes on new forms and expressions as it moves and cycles over time and humanity transforms.

As nations are formed out of the minds and activities of higher beings, Steiner describes complex relationships of the higher beings who work

---

[36] Steiner, Rudolf. The Mystery of Death. Lecture. Prague, 13th May 1915

within their planes and, in turn, influence and interact with the divine beings beneath them to accomplish certain tasks. A quality or aspect, as an impulse, for humanity flows down through the hierarchy during certain points of our evolution. Each Spirit of the Age, whom Steiner describes as exalted beings and inspirers, govern in successive time periods and place a particular stamp, or goal, upon humanity over the course of vast epochs of time. [37]

> "These Spirits of Personality, these inspirers of the Spirit of the Age, are of a higher order than the Folk Spirits. In every epoch one of these Spirits of Personality is predominant and sets his seal upon the whole epoch, assigns to the Folk Spirits their specific tasks, so that the whole spirit of the epoch is determined by the special or individual characteristics of the Folk Spirit. Then, in the following epoch, another Spirit of Personality, another of the Archai, takes over."[38]

One aspect of the Archangel Michael's task is to bring to humanity knowledge of the spiritual worlds as he does battle, as it were, with the opposing powers who seek to deprive humanity of our spiritual vision and direct knowledge of the spiritual worlds. Michael's task in the current age is to bring activity and movement into humanity so that we can take a step closer to the spiritual worlds and direct knowledge of the Christ. Michael brings clarity and insight while the opposing powers, which shall be reviewed in the next section, seek to confuse and polarize us. Michael is the herald and the bringer of the Christ as a global transformational impulse.

According to Steiner, a victory was achieved that was led by Michael over a group of demonic beings that began in 1840 and concluded in the year 1879. These beings had, in fact, up to that point been working in alignment with the spirit of the age and their proper task. When that task expired and evolved, they refused to evolve too and thus were cast out of the spiritual worlds into the spiritual-earthbound plane where they walk amongst humanity today in a coordinated, meddlesome, and more personal way.

---

[37] There is clearly a divine mystery with regards to how spiritual impulses flow into the human being that has not been perceived the author. Consult Dr. Steiner's research for further study.

[38] Steiner, Rudolf. The Mission of the Individual Folk-Souls, Lecture 1. Angels, Folk Spirits, Time Spirits: their part in the Evolution of Mankind.

This group of opposing beings stood against the Christ's, and Michael's, task to bring to human beings a direct path, bridge, and knowledge of the spiritual worlds preferring to rather to continue with their tasks after their apportioned time of influence had come to an end.

Left: "Michael" by artist Baron Arild von Rosenkrantz (1870-1964) who created many paintings in the anthroposophical spiritual stream and made contributions to the 1st Goetheanum in Dornach, Switzerland that was destroyed by arson in 1922. The Archangel Michaél, as a messenger of the Christ impulse and the leader of the seven Archangels, is the leader or "regent" of the current age of humanity that began in 1879 and shall continue for 300-400 years.[39]

Steiner confirmed and revealed that the Archangels guide humanity in regencies of 300-400 years and the seven leading Archangels comprise a cycle of 2,160 years (354x7 cycles) that equates to one "house" of the zodiac. Michael's 300–400-year regency began in 1879. This coincided with a necessary spiritual dark age that is referred to in spiritual science as "Kali Yuga" that was coming to an end (began in about 3000BC and ended in 1899AD) and a fresh impulse for humanity was delivered out of the spiritual worlds. This new spiritual impulse, as brought forth by the Christ and Michael, is one reason why we see spiritual movements and genuine leaders emerge in the West, such as Rudolf Steiner, during the 18th-20th centuries in a public way.

Michael, as described by Rudolf Steiner is a cosmopolitan being who works through human beings and therefore does not take on human form. The

---

[39] "It has been granted to me to feel a breath of the realization that beyond this world of toil and sorrow and pleasure there are worlds in which Beings who have never come to earth as men yet watch and guide us all." Baron Arild von Rosenkrantz, A New Impulse in Art, Page 11.

notions of race, gender, nationality, or group-based aspects that divide human beings and pit them against one another work against his, and the Christ's, mission. Like the Christ and the divine beings who exist above human beings, Michael stands above the egotism of humanity.

While the beings of the Spiritual Hierarchies work collaboratively and in alignment with the will of God, some beings stand in opposition. Christ, the Spiritual Hierarchies, and the divine messengers who work through human beings and the leaders of humanity do battle with these beings who, like the divine Spiritual Hierarchies, align themselves under principal leaders. The divine beings of the hierarchies allow the opposing powers to operate as they occupy a proper place in the cosmos and bring constructive benefits to humanity. Dr. Steiner reveals that the world would not exist without them. Thus, a battle rages within human beings who bring either divine influences or the impulses of the opposing beings into the outer world.

It is only when one allows one's self to slip into a polarizing influence, or exacerbation, of the opposing powers that problems arise. Steiner provides many insightful details regarding the nature and the influences of the opposing powers who seek to pull humanity in one of two opposing directions, both of which are out of alignment with the will of the Christ, the balance of the human being, and the right path of human transformation. Many of these beings have been remained behind, having not progressed, during prior phases of human evolution and while their sphere of activity has evolved, their core task and being remains the same.

Understanding the true nature of these opposing forces, at least at a high level, is critical to laying a proper foundation for an understanding of the true nature of Joan of Arc's mission for she was a genuine leader and messenger working on behalf of higher beings. Working through the Folk Soul of France, Joan received direction and instructions from angelic guides whom she described as St. Michael, St. Gabriel, St. Margaret, and St. Catherine. Joan was vital to setting a proper course, or realignment, as it were, to humanity through the French nation. A course and predestined change to humanity, as planned by the hierarchies, was at risk of not coming into fulfillment due to the influences of the opposing powers who had inspired human beings in a certain way for some time before Joan's incarnation.

It was Joan who, having worked through a coordinated plan with the divine beings who oversee our development before being born, achieved the desired outcome that set things right again. That could only be accomplished by separating France from England and thus achieving French liberty by pushing the English out of France and Europe. As a result, both countries brought to humanity their unique cultural influences and the proper path of global transformation.

Aspect 2: The Opposing Powers of Ahriman and Lucifer

The mighty divine beings who oversee humanity are engaged in a perpetual battle with the opposing powers. This struggle continues perpetually concerning the proper path for the transformation of humanity. Except for the few who have achieved a genuine spiritual bridge and vision, most of humanity in modern times has descended into a form of blindness and amnesia. While this transition through amnesia is a path that humanity is required to pass through, it is the result of the activities and influences of the opposing powers who work within the planned course of evolution for the human being. Humanity is just now emerging out of a necessary spiritual dark age, or "Kali Yuga", that ended in 1899 that was essential for humanity's development when, as Dr. Steiner reveals, it was necessary to transform the human being in a new way. As a result, the vast majority of us have lost any direct knowledge of the Spiritual Hierarchies and thus, the powers who oppose them have become lost to our perception.

Therefore, it is critical to understand, at least at a high level, who these beings are and how they relate to humanity. Dr. Steiner, as a genuine spiritual initiate, brought direct knowledge of these beings forward to humanity as part of the Christ's and Michael's mission in the modern age. As the construct of humanity transforms and the world with it, the ways that the Christ, Michael, and the hierarchies approach man also evolve. There is a balance that needs to be achieved between the opposing forces and the benefits that they bring to humanity as overseen by higher beings. For the human being who lives within the conditions of the world that are the direct outcomes of the activities of higher beings, and the influences of the opposing powers, achieving balance requires insight, activity, foresight, and engagement.

This is especially important in any study of the events of history, and in particular the life of Joan of Arc, because she worked collaboratively with divine beings who represent the Spiritual Hierarchies, as led by the Christ, to offset a crisis that had come into being at the 15th century. This crisis emerged as a result of the influences of the opposing powers who are perpetually at work in diverse ways. Joan's life and mission manifested outwardly in a political and military task, that was the necessary playing field upon which the separation of France from England had to occur. England's imperialistic ambitions, exacerbated by egotism, were threatening to absorb France and thus a crisis emerged that threatened to interrupt the proper cultural development of the countries of Europe and the impulses that these cultures would bring to the world.

According to Steiner, during the 14th and 15th centuries, the opposing forces had influenced a certain imbalance through the English nation that threatened to annihilate the French nation, and thus her cultural impulse and proper place in the world. As all nations are connected as a global family, a change in the French cultural direction at that moment in time would have led to catastrophic consequences for humanity.[40] Had the opposing powers intervened successfully, this transformational impulse that was being brought to humanity per the will of the higher divine beings could have been prevented thus leading humanity into a state of corruption and imbalance.

As Steiner reveals, the battle between the opposing influences and the Divine is not dualistic as is traditionally represented in religion and theology. This is revealed in a conflict between Satan, the Devil, or Lucifer, and God, the Creator, and/or Christ. This battle is sometimes presented in materialistic and illusory terms as God vanquishing the Devil and thus evil is destroyed. In reality, as Steiner reveals through his expanded powers of clairvoyance, there are two principal and opposing beings and influences at work from the spiritual worlds and not just one. These polarized beings exist as two opposing extremes pushing and pulling the human being out of balance. Balance is only achieved by identifying, managing, and properly transforming the influences of the opposing powers.

This balance is achieved through the Christ and the higher beings who support His mission. The opposing beings, who are supported by a hierarchy of supporting beings loyal to their cause, seek to corrupt and polarize the human being into a state of permanent imbalance. They wish to distort the human being into caricature, as it were, of what we should be in the mind of God and the divine beings who bring His will, and Word, into the world. If the opposing beings have their way, we become slaves and servants of their missions. The Christ seeks freedom for humanity and each human being is a part of a global community. The opposing beings seek to

---

[40] Refer to the transition of the evolution of the Intellectual Soul to the Consciousness or Spiritual Soul in Rudolf Steiner's body of knowledge including World History in the light of Anthroposophy, Lecture VII. This new aspect of human consciousness is contemplated throughout this work.

accomplish this eternal task in an evolving and dynamic way over long periods of time. Thus, acquiring genuine knowledge of the spheres of their activity is critical to overcoming and managing their influences so that one can rise above them.

As Steiner reveals, the opposing influences lead a cast of supporting beings who carry out their will in a variety of ways. They are known as "Ahriman" and "Lucifer".[41] These two beings and their coworkers exist within, and work out of, the spiritual worlds. They are not physical beings. However, these two leaders, and their subordinates, influence individuals and groups in the physical world through our inner being whether we are aware of it or not. In fact, the opposing beings prefer to project their influences into humanity anonymously thus making their efforts all the more effective. As was Steiner's task, and is the quest of genuine spiritual knowledge, by revealing the activities of these opposing beings one can then effectively identify and manage their influences. In historical terms, one can then properly review history and the past in terms of how the Spiritual Hierarchies and the opposing influences worked through human beings at any given moment, thus influencing the course of human destiny.

On one polarity exists a group of subsensible beings known as "Ahriman" that are the spirits of false pride and materialism. They are referred to by Dr. Steiner as the "Spirit of Darkness" who "through imperfection and evil, brings shadows into the light."[42] This group seeks to pull humanity towards the earth into all things solid, physical, and three-dimensional. Ahriman's influences seek to corrupt the human being into a one-sided dependency on the intellect and the outer world. Thus, these beings steer one towards materialism and a perception that is devoid of valid spiritual ideas. If spiritual ideas manifest, Ahriman will seek to corrupt the environment by inspiring illusions or pitting one perspective against the other. Ahriman grabs hold of the power of the intellect through rigid and materialistic thinking. This does not mean that thought, or thinking, is improper. The power of thinking, through the human "I", is the means by which we are led to true spiritual freedom. It is a key aspect of humanity that was

---

[41] As revealed by Rudolf Steiner. These terms are inherited names from religious texts; however, I use them with regards to the anthroposophical source as brought forth by Dr. Steiner. The name "Ahriman" is derived from Manichaeism and is predicated upon the working construct of the opposing forces of light and dark in the universe. It is carried forward by Steiner to describe a specific higher being and its influences.
[42] Steiner, Rudolf, Turning Points Spiritual History, Part I, Zarathustra, Six Lectures, January 1911 – January 1912.

brought to us by the Archangel Michael through the Christ and the Spiritual Hierarchies. Right thinking, as a Christ and Michael impulse, is based on objectivity, a true perception of the spirit, the soul, freedom, love, life, brotherhood, and a genuine bridge to the spiritual worlds. It is the enabler of individual freedom. Ahriman seeks to rob humanity of spiritual perception and thus the presence of spiritual truths, principles, and the higher beings that created and sustain the physical world. Thus, we lose freedom, power, and insight. Ahriman wants to bond human beings to the earth in a physical way and deprive us of our connection to the spiritual worlds.

Ahrimanic beings are confined to the subsensible realms and live directly amongst humanity in the spiritual-earthbound plane where they seek to influence and enslave an unsuspecting humanity to their will. Ahriman's goal is a world devoid of culture, art, spiritual ideas, and spiritual insights. War, crude instincts, division, conflict, and situations where people are opposed to one another based on lower impulses, race, nationality, religion, culture, gender, or any group-based quality that sets one against another are, at least in part, influenced by the activities of Ahrimanic beings. Ahrimanic beings heavily influence the instinctual impulses through the metabolism of the human being.

> "They influence instincts, desires, and passions. They live directly upon the earth, yet in a way that is invisible to people. They possess only a body that lives in the essence of earth and water."[43]

At the present moment, Ahriman seeks to project the illusion into humanity that a materialistic observation is, in fact, the only reality and that there is no inner spiritual meaning behind a physical object. Observing a planet, for example, and suggesting that it rotates around the sun over a certain period of time and at a certain rate due to purely gravitational, physical, or mathematical reasons with no inner reason or purpose that is connected to the Spiritual Hierarchies, is an Ahrimanic observation. Ahriman can project cold and stilling influences through the intellect but he is also attached to the earth. One of Ahriman's goals is a complete

---

[43] Steiner, Rudolf, <u>Spirit as Sculptor of the Human Organism</u>, <u>Sixteen Lectures Given in Stuttgart, Dornach</u>, The Hague, London and Berlin in 1922, CW 218.

hardening of the human being devoid of any spiritual activity. In Ahriman, lies the "origin of the aberrations of thought."[44]

An iterative model sculpture of "Ahriman" by Rudolf Steiner and Edith Maryon.[45]

Dr. Steiner reveals that, conversely, there exists a group of beings who collectively unite under a single leader known as "Lucifer". Steiner states in his lectures that Ahriman, and not Lucifer, comes closer to the contemporary perception of "Satan" and the "Devil". The traditional conceptions of Lucifer as a being who lives beneath the earth as a mighty red devil with hooves, horns, a pitchfork, and a tail are illusory.

While Ahriman drags humanity down towards the earth and Lucifer seeks to pull humanity away from the earth. On the extreme, Lucifer's influences can lead to fantasies, dreams, unrestrained passions, and illusions that can lead to illness and death.[46] Narcissism, self-indulgence, and self-importance are the result of Luciferic influences. Like Ahriman, Luciferic beings seek to enslave humanity based on a kind of liberation from the Spiritual Hierarchies and independence from the physical world. The proper ordering of humanity's constitution, and state of balance, falls within the collective hierarchy of the divine higher beings of which humanity has its rightful path and proper place. One of Lucifer's goals is to disrupt that alignment and bring humanity exclusively under his domain.

> "The Luciferic principle strives to make every human being independent, to endow the single individual with the greatest

---

[44] Steiner, Rudolf, The Luciferic and Ahrimanic in Relation to Man, Article from the journal, Das Reich, Volume 3, Number 3.

[45] This image is a realistic portrait, and not a caricature, of Ahriman as revealed by the supersensible perception of Rudolf Steiner and confirmed by the author's direct experience.

[46] Steiner reveals that breathing and digestive problems follow one who gives into the passions, as inspired by Lucifer, from one life to the next.

possible power."[47] Yet, these beings also seek to rob humanity of our freedom as they "hate human freedom above all else and wish to have nothing to do with it."[48]

Thus, on the Luciferic extreme, the powers of egotism, passions, vanity, self-importance, and independence are amplified. To say that Lucifer makes exclusive use of the passions, however, is not correct. It appears from Steiner's extensive lectures on the subject state that both Ahrimanic and Luciferic beings make use of the passions, or lower instinctual impulses, to suit their own ends depending on the conditions and needs of the moment. Perhaps one could say that instinctual impulses arise from the earth, through self-preservation and the base needs of purely physical reproduction, while the passions, through egotism, influence one into a state of perversion, narcissism, and decadence. People are flung from one polarity to the other as these two beings work in collaboration with one another as it suits their goals at any given moment in time.

> "Luciferic spirits are also present today and these prefer to attack man from within. They want to generate all kinds of passions, but not the error of the intellect, the error of common reason that we have to struggle with in our present age."[49] "...for all that is imparted in the way of spiritual-scientific concepts refers to the higher worlds, not to the world in which Lucifer aims to stimulate man's interest, not to the sense world alone."[50]

Either group can stir up, exacerbate, and excite the passions, desires, and emotions that have their root in the astral, or feeling, body of the human being in an effort to overheat the blood and generate imbalance.[51] Dr. Steiner also reveals that these two influences are not inherently detrimental and that they also bring constructive aspects to human evolution. For example, Lucifer brings a conception of the arts and the impulse of individual freedom which, if corrupted, can lead one away from

---

[47] Steiner, Rudolf, The Gospel of St. Matthew, Lecture III, November 23, 1909.

[48] Steiner, Rudolf, Spirit as Sculptor of the Human Organism, Sixteen Lectures Given in Stuttgart, Dornach, The Hague, London and Berlin in 1922, CW 218.

[49] Steiner, Rudolf. The Destinies of Individuals and Nations. Lecture 5, The Nature of the Christ Impulse and the Michaelic Sprit Serving It.

[50] Steiner, Rudolf. The Gospel of St. John. Lecture VI. GA112.

[51] Refer to the lectures and writings of Rudolf Steiner regarding the sheaths, or layers, of the human being of which the astral body is an essential aspect. The astral body, or sheath, is the source of the feeling aspects of the human being.

balance and the Christ. Ahriman influences the use of the intellect. The relationship between these opposing beings and influences is, perhaps, difficult to comprehend in totality as they relate to each other, and the world, in a variety of ways based on the conditions of the age in which we live through spiritual pathways within the human being. In turn, these influences directly affect the individual human being. In centuries past, as Steiner reveals, Luciferic impulses were dominant at certain points of history as was the case during the time of Joan of Arc although Ahrimanic influences were also present.

Steiner reveals that Joan was perfectly suited for her spiritual and global task at that moment in time because she was impervious to the excessive Luciferic impulses of pride, egotism, and the passions that were prevalent at that time. Joan had purged these lower aspects from her being prior to her birth. So, to think soundly in spiritual-historical terms, a researcher should approach historical events in terms of what influences were dominant and thus acquire a more robust understanding of the transformative struggle that was occurring. In the modern age, Steiner reveals that Ahrimanic influences are prevalent and shall grow in intensity as time moves on.

Clever, hardened, rigid, philistine, instinctual, and prosaic. These terms were also used by Steiner used to describe the goal of Ahrimanic beings for humanity. Another perspective of Ahriman's relationship to humanity reveals that:

> "...what is the aim of these other beings, who build their strongholds immediately below the surface of the Earth, and whose activities rise up into man's metabolism, — for the phenomena we observe in the tides and less frequently in volcanic eruptions and earthquakes are always present also in the ebb and flow in man's metabolism. Whilst the Luciferic spirits build, as we said, their strongholds in the air, in order to fight for the moral — as against the earthly — element in man, the Ahrimanic beings struggle to harden man; they want to make him like themselves."[52]

So, Ahrimanic and Luciferic beings are viewed properly as spiritual beings that bring forth certain constructive forces and, on the extreme, can lead

---

[52] Steiner, Rudolf. The Planetary Spheres and Their Influence on Man's Life on Earth and in Spiritual Worlds, Lecture 5, London, November 16, 1922.

to destructive impulses. For example, explosions of passion and temperament are connected either to Luciferic or Ahrimanic impulses and give rise to physical disorders and illnesses. While Ahriman would prefer that humanity remain permanently bound to the physical earth, Lucifer would prefer that souls do not incarnate into the physical plane, which is the dominion of Ahriman. So, while in Ahriman lies the error of thought, in Lucifer lies the "erring of will."[53] Lucifer can incite the emotions, feelings, and the blood to be inflamed that can inspire bursts of egotism and the fiery passions. The quest for egotism and power, for example, in whatever field of activity it finds expression, is a result of Luciferic influences. Therefore,

> "...we have thus around us in our earthly environment two hosts of beings; one in the air, that wants to make man moral but to lift him away from the Earth, and then we have also, immediately below the surface of the Earth, the Ahrimanic beings who want to draw man down and fasten him permanently to the Earth..."[54]

In another lecture, Steiner reveals that:

> "Lucifer is the power that stirs up in man all fanatical, all falsely mystical forces, all that physiologically tends to bring the blood into disorder and so lift man above and outside himself. Ahriman is the power that makes man dry, prosaic, philistine — that ossifies him and brings him to the superstition of materialism. And the true nature and being of man is essentially the effort to hold the balance between the powers of Lucifer and Ahriman; the Christ Impulse helps present humanity to establish this equilibrium."[55]

---

[53] Ibid.

[54] Ibid.

[55] Steiner, Rudolf. The Ahrimanic Deception. Lecture, Zurich, October 27, 1919. By "Philistine", Steiner may mean a person who wishes to remain static and not change or transform. It should be confused with a biblical term. In addition, it should be considered that not all Luciferic or Ahrimanic influences are inherently negative. These influences become negative only when they work against the appropriate transformative impulse for humanity at any given moment in time or a human being becomes exacerbated by them and falls out of balance. As Steiner demonstrated, the goal is not to destroy or despise these forces but to seek and achieve balance through the middle way, which is Christ.

"Lucifer" from the sculpture "Representative of Humanity" by Rudolf Steiner and Edith Maryon.

So, through Dr. Steiner, we gain profound insights into the true nature of the spiritual worlds in the modern age. One can form a balanced and informed perspective of the opposing forces. These forces cannot be destroyed but only identified, managed, and regulated in our daily lives. These polarized forces can be overcome and utilized in a human being's experience in a constructive way. If the influences of these beings grab hold of us in flashes of unawareness as exacerbated by the conditions upon which one is born into the world, we can become servants of their self-interest and fall into error. Only through education and knowledge of these beings can one begin to manage their influences and thus achieve healthy transformation and balance.

While both groups provide necessary and constructive influences to humanity, they exist in the field of polarities and thus attempt to steer humanity into behaviors and activities that ultimately serve their own aims to the extreme. They do not exist or work in a balanced way nor do they seek the proper balance of humanity. Attempts to rationalize the manifestations of these corrupted, or evil, influences into a purely psychological foundation is an Ahrimanic deception. The Christ, as the redeemer of humanity, provides a path for this balance and an awareness of the proper constitution of the human being given the various influences that bombard us from one moment to the next, one experience to the next, and one age to the next.

The Christ, and those that serve him, compel a seeking soul to identify and manage these polarities and achieve balance and thus, proper growth and development. We can each learn to identify, manage, and slay one's inner dragons that we, over time, have given birth inside our souls by falling under the influences of the opposing forces. Each human being is a composition of hidden spiritual beings, and thus influences, and are therefore unique and peculiar based on one's disposition and soul-history.

The battle for the human being, and one's soul, is disregarded at our peril. Ignoring the existence and influences of these beings inevitably compels one to fall into traps, mistakes, and snares. While the higher beings who oversee humanity continually intercede on our behalf, it is up to each human being to motivate themselves and learn about the influences of the opposing forces in order to manage, control, and channel one's activities, thoughts, and deeds properly.

> "...a fearful war is waged all the time between the air-fire beings (Lucifer) and the earth-water beings (Ahriman); they fight to get possession of man. And it is important that man should be aware of this war that is perpetually being waged for him; he must not be blind to it."[56]

The results of the influences of the opposing powers do not end in the physical world. Steiner further reveals that the Ahrimanic powers seek to extend the attachment of human beings to the physical world beyond death and into a supersensible existence where spiritual beings, who have no physical body, are permanently bound to the earth. Dr. Steiner reveals that when Ahrimanic beings successfully influence a human being into a dissolute life governed by the passions and crude instincts, then they make use of the spiritual outcomes of that activity in a tangible way. They do this with the goal of creating a race of subsensible slave-beings who will inhabit the spiritual earth-bound plane so they can be used to serve Ahriman's interests.

> "Suppose a man has strong and rude instincts. These beings (Ahrimanic) will clutch at his instinctive nature and seize hold of it. The man then falls victim to the Ahrimanic powers. He is completely given up to his passions and leads a wild and dissolute life. When a man has in this way become a prey, during his earthly life, to the Ahrimanic powers, then these powers will be able to hold on to his instinctive nature and tear it out of him after death. There exists already on the Earth a whole population of beings who have arisen in this way. They are there, in the elements of earth and water, a sub-human race."[57]

---

[56] Ibid. This is an abridged quote. Parenthesis is the author's.

[57] So, it appears that as Lucifer inspires the passions which inflames the feeling aspect of the human being while Ahriman inspires rude and instinctual impulses that also have an adverse

So, the opposing beings of the Christ, and the Spiritual Hierarchies, always work with corruptive intentions in each of us, and yet we cannot avoid their influences. Human beings can never "defeat" or "eliminate" their influences in a traditional materialistic sense. One must learn to understand and necessarily resist the polarizing influences of these spiritual beings and therefore manage them properly. With time, effort, and patience, one can strengthen the will and spiritual shield of our being to take only that which is useful and appropriate at any given moment. We can build resistance and utilize the influences of the opposing beings through the knowledge of the spiritual world brought to us by the Christ, Michael, and the teachings of the great leaders of humanity so that we can become impervious and resilient to hostile forces and influences.

> "To this day there has been much talk about Christianity and the Christ impulse, but man has not yet gained a clear understanding of what the Christ impulse has brought into the world as the result of the Mystery of Golgotha. Certainly, it is generally admitted that there is a Lucifer or an Ahriman, but in so doing, it is made to appear that from these two one must flee, as if one wished to say, "I want nothing to do with Lucifer and Ahriman!" — In yesterday's public lecture, I described the way in which the divine-spiritual forces can be found. If these forces did not want to have anything to do with Lucifer and Ahriman, either, the world could not exist. One does not gain the proper relationship to Lucifer and Ahriman by saying, "Lucifer, I flee from you! Ahriman, I flee from you!" Rather, everything that man has to strive for as a result of the Christ impulse must be seen as similar to the equilibrious state of a pendulum."[58]

This battle must be carefully monitored by the individual as the opposing forces are perpetually active and seek to create, foster, and find new and

---

effect in a similar way, but through a different path. Thus, there forms an over-reliance on the astral body, and the inflaming of the passions and feelings, which in turn are driven largely by the outer senses and egotism. The effect of these bestial and primal impulses that arise out of the uncontrolled passions are utilized by Ahrimanic beings to create a sub-human race of beings who are attached to the spiritual earthbound plane who are then pressed into a form of slavery by Ahrimanic beings who use them in an ongoing effort to corrupt humanity.

[58] Steiner, Rudolf. Christ in Relation to Lucifer and Ahriman. Linz, May 18, 1915. The comment "yesterday's lecture" refers to Supersensible Perception and Its Strengthening Soul-force in Our Time of Destiny.

innovative ways to disrupt, corrupt, and steer humanity away from the Christ, Michael, and our appropriate transformative path. They frequently inspire and utilize illusions that are fostered through the inner forces of thinking, feeling, and willing. Thus, these influences can appear to be quite real. The influences of the opposing beings inspire and exacerbate the vices of the human being which are amplified by things such as substance abuse, alcohol, and addictions. By seeking out genuine knowledge about the Spiritual Hierarchies and the opposing forces in a genuine and informed manner, we can thus be well-armed and achieve a balanced path.

Sometimes the opposing powers collaborate but more often than not they work at cross-purposes. Dr. Steiner reveals that the temptation of Christ, for example, was not undertaken by one being known as "Satan", but rather by the two opposing beings.[59] Steiner reveals that Christ Jesus was able to identify each of these beings according to their true natures and address and combat them properly. It is important to consider that opposing beings are higher beings who live within the eternal. They do not expire as human beings do in a physical way. They work through human beings. If a human being allows themselves to be polarized in her or his lifetime, then those influences will follow into the next and thus continue forward as a recurring aspect of one's being.

Thus, the opposing beings, or entities, stand against the Christ and the higher divine beings who work on humanity's behalf. The opposing beings stand as veritable kings, and leaders, above hierarchies of lower beings who serve them diligently, loyally, and vehemently. The opposing beings are as ancient as the world itself and have mastered the art of illusion, deception, and the insidious paths upon which humanity can best be led astray, most of which we are not aware of or are taught to observe properly through traditional education. They have, in modern times, successfully led many human beings into the realm of amnesia and delusion, and thus conceal their very existence.

To understand the true nature of the Christ, Michael, and the guiding beings of humanity, who seek to provide a productive transformational influence on human beings, and those who oppose the Christ one must turn to a deeper study that is outside the scope of this work. I recommend

---

[59] Refer to The Fifth Gospel and Christ in Relation to Lucifer and Ahriman lecture series by Rudolf Steiner.

reviewing the lectures of Rudolf Steiner, Ita Wegman,[60] and the leading members of the early Anthroposophical Society who wrote insightful works on the task of the Christ and Michael in the modern age. The Archangel Michael, who is sometimes appropriately referred to as the Sun-Hero in esoteric studies, is an important task not just for humanity but also for a better understanding of Joan's task and her spiritual mission for she, and those who were connected to her task, are in the service of Christ, Michael, and the divine higher beings who support and bring forth His mission on behalf of humanity.

In conclusion, Ahrimanic and Luciferic influences over time have brought benefits to humanity, but they primarily serve a role that opposes balance through the Christ, Michael, and the Spiritual Hierarchies and, as a result, have exercised a certain influence in varying ways, and intensities, upon humanity. In doing so, the opposing powers attempt to thwart the progress of mankind by bringing things ahead too soon, delaying things, or throwing things off track. The Christ, and the Spiritual Hierarchies, show humanity the right path by leading us into balance, redemption, and thus transformation.

It was through the activities of Luciferic beings, whose influences had become intensified in the 15th century, that a global crisis arose that was centered in France. To defeat the effects of the opposing powers, as a representative for a larger task and the Spiritual Hierarchies, the higher beings brought someone forth who would work on their behalf and help them to overcome the adverse effects that had manifested in the outer world and thus, set the path of Europe and the world right course again. That person was the soul who became Joan of Arc.

---

[60] Refer to Dr. Ita Wegman's work. On the Work of the Archangel Michael originally published as Aus Michaels Wirken in German for a deeper study of Michael's task. There are also a series of lectures concerning the Archangel Michael's task and role in humanity delivered by Rudolf Steiner.

Left: "The Representative of Humanity" by Rudolf Steiner and Edith Maryon. This sculpture is on display at the Goetheanum in Dornach, Switzerland. In this portrayal, Christ stands triumphant as the Representative of Humanity over Lucifer (above) and Ahriman (below). Christ's victory represents a perfect balance between the two opposing influences. Note, Ahriman and Lucifer have not been vanquished with weapons, as we see in some forms of art, in this portrayal. The two polarities, or beings, have been properly identified and managed through the power of Christ's being, power, knowledge, and balance.

Left: Rudolf Steiner in the workshop studio near the Goetheanum in Dornach, Switzerland. Below: Edith Maryon (1872-1924).

Aspect 3: The Masters, Initiates, Messengers, and Spiritual Initiation

Some souls incarnate in the physical world who are very highly developed and spiritually mature. They have progressed far beyond the rest of humanity as they have deliberately and consistently pursued the proper path of spiritual transformation over time. They work directly for the higher divine beings who guide humanity. They are known by names such as "Initiates", "Divine Messengers", and "Masters". There is a council of 12 leaders, or "Bodhisattvas", who work as a college and represent the bridge between higher beings and humanity. They incarnate in the physical and spiritual world in a regular cadence to bring the divine mission into the physical world. These masters comprise a body of individuals who serve as an active bridge to the divine. They lead critical spiritual missions and tasks for humanity. They operate anonymously and are unknown to the masses. As is required, the great masters and leaders have coworkers, delegates, and messengers who work on their behalf, either knowingly or unknowingly, to accomplish a mission for humanity.

There is a process at work for those who choose to pursue the deliberate transformative path of the human soul that requires commitment, dedication, sacrifice, training, purification, and transformation. This transformative process is known historically as spiritual initiation. It is not a passive or holistic process. It is achieved only with the assistance of the Christ, higher beings including Angels, the Bodhisattvas, and those who serve them who oversee the development of the human being. The masters form a global community of fellows, as it were, and are genuine, authorized, and proven leaders of humanity. Some of the names of these high leaders have surfaced in the public eye over time and some of their names were revealed by Rudolf Steiner as was appropriate for his task.[61]

Supporting the great mission of the Spiritual Hierarchies are teams of people who work together, as guided by higher beings and masters, who work to achieve a common purpose separated by various geographies and cultures. In the ancient world, individuals who were determined to be

---

[61] I recommend The Mission of Christian Rosenkreutz by Rudolf Steiner, Rudolf Steiner and the Masters of Esoteric Christianity by Sergei O. Prokofieff, Esoteric Development, The Great Initiates, Chapter VII by Rudolf Steiner, and The Great Initiates by Édouard Schuré for further research. Rudolf Steiner's body of knowledge contains multiple lectures and references to the task of the Great Initiates and how that task has evolved over time. There are many others, but Edgar Cayce also provides some insights on the Masters.

sufficiently prepared and ready for initiation were trained in "mystery centers", such as Ephesus that was active during the Greek period. The initiates were called by many names including masters, high-priests, magicians, teachers, hierophants, etc. The time of the initiates in the ancient world, and those who have achieved initiation throughout history, are not to be confused with pretenders and those who borrow terms and vernacular to suit their own financial and vain self-interest in the modern world. This area of study is filled with superstitions regarding the existence of these highly developed people and the higher beings they serve.

Throughout history, the hidden aspects of life, humanity, and our relationship to the spiritual worlds were taught only by those who could form and maintain a genuine bridge to the spiritual worlds and thus perceive them properly. All genuine spiritual initiates possess deep and penetrating inner insights that are the results of expanded powers of clairvoyance that are the natural byproduct of the maturation and evolution of the human soul. The human soul, like the physical body, is a living organism that transforms with applied effort, will, and direction. This transformation is only the result of dedication, commitment, training, and sacrifice across *repeated* lifetimes. The powers and maturity of the initiate far surpass the average human being who relies purely on the physical senses, instincts, and intellect. Most of us have pursued the path of gradual, or holistic, transformation and thus our spiritual capabilities and potential lie in a dormant state, as it were. It is because of this reality that the majority of human beings are blind to the facts of the spiritual worlds and those who serve broader missions on behalf of humanity. It is because of the threat of the opposing powers in the modern age that this must change.

In times long past, the hidden aspects of human existence were revealed only to the candidates for spiritual initiation, or the those who passed through the membrane of spiritual initiation, in the ancient mystery centers who went through long, arduous, planned, and challenging cycles of discipline, training, and preparation in special training facilities and temples that were designed specifically for the purpose of expedited spiritual education and transformation. This long and exhaustive transformative process, which followed strict rules and took place in a concentrated form in an isolated and protected facility, was personally observed and facilitated by genuine spiritual masters, or master-initiates, who could appropriately and responsibly oversee the testing and transformation of each individual who was always unique.

This intimate relationship was predicated upon knowing, in detail, the inner being of each person and advising upon an individual's unique attributes, soul-history, and personal strengths and weaknesses. It is, perhaps, the most personal of relationships and is based on perfect trust and guidance. In the ancient mystery centers, the final test for the candidate for initiation occurred over a 3 ½ day "temple sleep" period where the individual entered the spiritual worlds, guided by the hierophant, leaving their physical body and passing through the planes of the higher worlds. If the candidate failed the tests or was unprepared, the outcome could be a diminution and contraction of consciousness, insanity, or perhaps even death. If the candidate returned successfully to his or her body after 3 ½ days, as the candidate was kept in a tomb in a death-like sleep that imitated the death experience that each person passes through at the end of our lives, he or she awakened as a transformed individual with greatly expanded faculties, insights, and capabilities that far exceeded those who trod the casual path of the outer world.[62]

In the ancient world, the truths and inner knowledge gained by the process of spiritual initiation were not known to the masses and were intentionally kept secret. In the modern world, previously hidden knowledge has been brought forth into the public domain through the activities of the initiates who, through the revelation of the Christ who is the living and omnipresent fulfillment of all of the ancient mysteries, seek to bring that knowledge to the public so that anyone can pursue, as an individual task, true spiritual freedom and transformation. It is an individual choice for each human being. This quest is overseen by the guiding spiritual leaders of humanity who work through the Christ. It is open to all who seek it with a genuine and good heart. It is a core aspect of one who is willing to embark upon this journey that consists, among other things, the purging of one's lower impulses and inner dragons that have influenced the soul over time and led to redemptive karma and life-patterns. This journey revolves around one's karma and how the invisible attributes that exist at the core of the human

---

[62] Refer to Dr. Steiner's Occult Science, an Outline. Also, refer to Ita Wegman's The Mysteries which provides some valuable insights. The book Initiation written by Elizabeth Haich provides a description of a spiritual initiation experience during a distant ancient period in Egypt where she was guided through the process of spiritual initiation. She discusses the tests, challenges, and prerequisites of that experience.

being have been exacerbated by the opposing beings or have found balance through the Spirit and the being of Christ-Jesus.

For a proper review of this expansive topic of spiritual study, I recommend turning to the authorities on these topics and those who should be consulted to build a proper foundation for esoteric studies in the modern era.[63] Understanding the construct and operative process of spiritual initiation is important because, as shall be discussed later on, Steiner revealed that Joan of Arc had passed through a unique form of spiritual transformation, or initiation, through the Christ before being born so that she could accomplish a greater mission on behalf of the world.[64]

---

[63] Such works can be found in the lectures of Rudolf Steiner and supporting Anthroposophical researchers who followed in his footsteps but elements of the mysteries can also be found in Edgar Cayce, the Theosophists, and the Rosicrucians.

[64] One must remember that Christ is a global impulse. It is not national or regional although He works when and where He chooses as is appropriate for His mission. Thus, when one observes that the Christ entered into someone as it did with Joan as shall be discussed throughout this work, it is with the intention of bringing forth a global impulse and not one limited by race, gender, nation, or culturál identity. This Christ impulse is a world impulse for all of humanity.

Aspect 4: Reincarnation and Karma

The ongoing process of spiritual transformation for humanity, and the human being, is not a blind process of coincidence, chance, or "luck". This process is overseen by higher divine beings, including our guardian angels, and it is interwoven with the forward momentum of time, seeking, transformation, grace, compassion, and love. This transformative impulse emanates out of higher beings, led by Christ Jesus, who oversees human development over time. One's name and form are temporary and are destined to come to an end in physical terms, yet the spiritual mission continues.[65] All beings, whether they are incarnate or discarnate, exist in a state of growth, change, and movement. Love is the binding element that created, sustains, and redeems human beings and the world.

The spiritual transformation of the individual and the world occurs only over long periods of time by way of the working operative principle of reincarnation, karma, and repeated earth lives. This mysterious process leads to redemption, growth, and development. The core premise and essence of this operative principle that binds one life to the next is karma and relationships. Karma is a fulfillment based on the free will and choices of the individual who, as discussed previously, are aided and influenced by higher beings who work for or against our proper transformation.

Therefore, understanding one's karmic history, and future, is a key aspect of the path of initiation and spiritual transformation. It is not, however, necessary to understand the importance of one's karmic history in order to grasp Joan's life and mission. It is sufficient to perceive that the soul who became Joan had a karmic history and served a broader purpose for humanity at that moment in time. Her soul was prepared by deliberate effort, accomplishments, sacrifices, and transformations. The destiny of nations, and how things had evolved through the activities of people led to a critical transformative point in the 15th century of which Joan's task was interwoven. If the events of the 15th century had not been set anew due to Joan's involvement the current and proper construct of the world would

---

[65] "In the epoch of the Consciousness Soul (the current epoch) we must develop a sense that the external events of history are subject to birth and death, and that, whatever we create, be it a child's toy or an empire, we create in the knowledge that it must one day perish. Failure to recognize the impermanence of things is irrational, just as it would be irrational to believe that one could bear a child which was entitled to live on earth forever." Steiner, Rudolf. From Symptom to Reality, Lecture 4.

not have occurred. Our transformative plan would have been corrupted, thus requiring further corrective actions and sacrifices, the substance and extent of which is not knowable in human terms.

Joan's mission was not a task that just anyone could have undertaken. She had, through long cycles of development and preparation, put herself in a position to be a proper vehicle for the fulfillment of the Christ impulse at that moment in time. Thus, Joan of Arc is not a simple child who heard mysterious voices and served purely a political purpose alone on behalf of France and King Charles VII and somehow got lucky along the way in the victories that she achieved over the English and Burgundians while leading the French army. Rather, Joan was an advanced and mature soul who had achieved a high degree of spiritual transformation and was enabled and supported by Christ-Jesus, and higher divine beings, on a global mission.

In terms of karmic histories, for example, Buddha revealed that he had lived some 555 or so lifetimes before becoming Buddha. A "Buddha" is a term used to describe an individual who achieves a series of advanced transformations through multiple spiritual initiations over a long period of time. Thus, Buddha achieved a very high degree of spiritual attainment and transformation. Steiner confirms that he did not return to a physical body after his death and now works exclusively from the spiritual worlds. Human beings live hundreds, and perhaps even thousands, of lifetimes. The perception of, and understanding thereabouts, one's past lives is a key aspect of the genuine spiritual seeker's path that unfolds gradually over time only with the help of the initiates, our guardian angels, spiritual guides, friends, and teachers who work through the Christ through the spiritual worlds.

In summary, karma, spiritual preparation, sacrifice, and destiny are key aspects of Joan's life and mission. The nature of Joan's specific karma is not the object of this study. The nature of karma, the influences that were brought about by higher beings and the opposing forces over time, and the mission and task for that moment in time for which Joan volunteered to take on, is a part of appreciating and contemplating the magnitude of her accomplishment. Joan came into the world knowing that she had a task to fulfill, observed it faithfully and objectively as it unfolded before her during her physical life within the confines and constraints of the physical world, accepted her mission, and fulfilled a broader task on behalf of humanity.

Aspect 5: The Akashic Records

The law of birth, life, death, and rebirth is karma and destiny. The entire soul-history of each individual is contained and preserved within a universal substance. The total record of a soul's experiences of repeated lifetimes is referred to by many names including "spiritual lineage" and "karmic history". Our spiritual lineage is an ongoing book for each of us. It is one's comprehensive soul-history that includes all of the cause-and-effect relationships that each of us has carried, and may still carry, within our souls every day of *each* of our lifetimes. This information, also sometimes referred to as the "cosmic script" during the Middle Ages, is imprinted upon the skein of space and time and is accessible to those who are granted access and are sufficiently mature to "read" it. The concept of a Great Hall of Records that resides in the spiritual worlds is an axiom, and basic principle, amongst spiritual and esoteric students as revealed by the initiates and genuine spiritual researchers. It is a comprehensive spiritual library and great hall of history that contains the all-inclusive history of actions, thoughts, feelings, and deeds of every soul in the universe.

By gaining access to this great hall of records, true spiritual insights have been provided by individuals who possessed an expanded degree of genuine clairvoyance and thus learned how to access and read from it. Dr. Rudolf Steiner is the leader in this regard as someone who could consciously and accurately read from the records. Others, such as Edgar Cayce, Madame Blavatsky, and hypnotic regression therapists have found a path to the records and published their findings thus revealing aspects of karma, humanity's cosmic history, relationships, circumstances, illness, dispositions, and the nuances of life. The terms "Hall of Records", "Akashic Records", "Cosmic Script", the "Secret Doctrine", and "Akasha-Essence" are synonymous terms that describe the same construct in the spiritual worlds.[66] Unfortunately, in modern times some people have grabbed hold of this idea and shaped it into a distorted concept.

The revelation of the Akashic Records gained prominence in America by way of Edgar Cayce and the Theosophists in the 20th century, however, preceding Edgar were the studies and lectures of Rudolf Steiner that were introduced to the world in German and, over time, have been translated into English and a host of languages. Steiner, as a high initiate, led the

---

[66] Steiner, Rudolf, Occult Science - An Outline, Part 4, Man and the Evolution of the World, Part I.

movement for genuine research and karmic relationships as gained through direct access to the Akashic Records.[67] It is only by accessing these records can the details of the true nature of history, individuals, the world, and human destiny be perceived and understood.[68] It was through the Akashic Records, or Akasha Essence as he sometimes referred to it, that Steiner brought forth details regarding Joan of Arc. The concept of the Book of Life, or the "book", is referred to in other places including the Book of Revelation in the Bible.

> "And I saw the dead, small and great, stand before God; and the books were opened: and another book was opened, which is the book of life: and the dead were judged out of those things which were written in the books, according to their works."[69]

It is also referred by Joan of Arc as reported in the Trial of Rehabilitation:

> "We often talked together, and I would say to her: "If you do not fear to go to the attack, it is because you know that you will not be killed": to which she would reply that she had no greater security than other soldiers. Sometimes Jeanne would tell me how she had been examined by the Clergy, and that she had made them the answer: "There are books of Our Lord's besides what you have."[70]

Contemporary historical studies are not capable of providing true insights into history. Historical studies provide insights, of course, but lack the inner spiritual realities behind historical events. The Akashic Records allow one to achieve an objective review of a historical event from all perspectives. Traditional researchers run into problems when they hypothesize and draw conclusions. In modern times, technology has enabled a finer review of historical events as they unfold, thus we can see what happened but certainly not the spiritual reality behind an event. So, understanding the inner nature of historical events, and people, remains hidden from our

---

[67] Refer to the Karmic Relationships and Cosmic Memory lecture cycles by Rudolf Steiner. Edgar Cayce also provided insights regarding karmic relationships and certain events of history through the Akashic Records and thus several books containing that phrase are in publication.

[68] There are no shortcuts to the Akashic Records.

[69] King James Version, Book of Revelation, 20:12.

[70] Steiner, Rudolf. The English translation of the trial files from 1902. From the book: Jeanne d'Arc Maid of Orléans Deliverer of France. Edited by T. Douglas Murray, Deposition of Dame Marguerite La Touroulde widow of the late Réné de Bouligny, Councillor to the King.

view regardless of it is the past or present. Therefore, when specific superficial details are known, they are helpful to know but they do not provide us with any genuine higher knowledge. For example, I can read the record of Joan's trial and learn details about her childhood, background, and habits, but know nothing of the true causes of her soul mission or the nuances of her being, appearance, and language. Therefore, as Steiner reveals, a true historical study can only be done through the Akashic Records and must consider the otherize hidden aspects. Historical research is a supporting aspect of genuine spiritual-historical research. It is only in that way that a spiritual investigator can verify findings, at least in a materialistic sense, that is the result of independent research.[71]

So, for the spiritual initiate and those who have access to the Akashic Records, an accurate detailed history on what occurred at any given moment of time throughout human history is available, and thus knowable. History can then be reviewed in a comprehensive multi-dimensional way. Very, very few researchers and individuals in the modern world have access to the Akashic Records consciously. Some, without knowing it, access the records subconsciously. Some hypnotic regression therapists have gained access to it but only through their patients and their patient's spiritual guides who work on their behalf. Edgar Cayce, for example, only gained access to the Hall of Records, which is a sacred construct, by way of a form of self-hypnosis that was the outcome of prior karma and a spiritual guardian who granted him access. It is from the Cosmic Script that Steiner was able to provide important details about Joan of Arc's lifetime by way of an expanded view of the past, the present, and the future. Not all of the details of Joan's life have been brought forward by Steiner...nor should they. It was, and is, not necessary for researchers to know all of the details of Joan's life, mission, and martyrdom.

Therefore, certain details are always protected by those who have access to the Akashic Records. Only aspects that are proper to reveal to the public have been brought forward by way of Rudolf Steiner who was bound by, and honored, an ethical and moral covenant as a high spiritual initiate. For the uninitiated or those who seek out the records with ulterior motives, the risk of exploitation is too great and thus access is restricted. Thus, the Akashic Records are a guarded aspect of spiritual research.

---

[71] In other words, spiritual researchers who have access to the Akashic Records will review historical documents and verify if a fact was correct or not. Historical records never take precedence for a mature spiritual-historical researcher.

Aspect 6: Christ-Jesus

Dr. Steiner provides deep insights with regards to Christ Jesus and the mystery of Golgotha that occurred in the year 30AD. It is not the intention of this work to provide a comprehensive study of Christ-Jesus because it is simply not feasible for the author. The event on Golgotha, and the mystery of the Christ, is the central defining evolutionary impulse for humanity. Thus, the scope of this work cannot provide a meaningful overview based on the author's limited knowledge and vision. The Christ's universal importance, role, and ongoing influences that He brings to the world and the human being are beyond the reckoning of any intellectual analysis. Therefore, I shall attempt only to provide a summary overview of the nature upon which the Christ, who is known as Christ-Jesus after Golgotha by Dr. Steiner. As revealed by Steiner, the Christ was a higher divine being who entered into the soul, through a spiritual event, of Joan before her birth and thus worked through her in the 15th century. These historical facts, as revealed through genuine spiritual perception as achieved by Steiner, shall be quoted and discussed as the reader moves through this study and not addressed in its entirety in this section.

The individual Christ-Jesus represents the balance between the two polarities of Ahriman and Lucifer and shows humanity the right path. He is the good shepherd, defender of the human being, and the permanent and designated life guide for each human being on the planet. The Christ is a higher divine being, the Sun-God and God of Light, who entered into Jesus during the baptism on the River Jordan in 30AD and brought to humanity a new impulse of transformation. The Christ perpetually brings His influences into the world to properly transform humanity and guide our progress appropriately. The Christ, as the Light of the World, came to humanity from the Sun-Sphere, which is the highest spiritual plane in the cosmos. Thus, He is a bringer of light in all of its forms including love, knowledge, freedom, awareness, balance, and life.

This lofty divine being known as the Christ, or the Sun-God, entered into the high spiritual initiate Jesus in 30AD and carried out a global and universal mission on behalf of humanity. It was the first and only time that this lofty spiritual being took on human form. The Christ, who merged with the man Jesus, is the redeemer of humanity who oversees our ongoing transformation from the spiritual worlds. Dr. Steiner refers to Christ-Jesus as "the Lord of Karma", the "Initiate of "Initiates", and the "Representative of Humanity". He is also sometimes referred to as the "13th disciple". This is important for obvious reasons, but it is especially pertinent to Joan's mission because, as was revealed by Rudolf Steiner, Joan's soul was transformed through a form of spiritual initiation before her birth where the Christ actively lived within her, albeit in a subconscious way during her lifetime, from that moment forward. Steiner tells us that it was the living being of the Christ working through her, and from within her, that enabled Joan to achieve the accomplishments at that moment in time that otherwise would not have been possible.

Before Golgotha, the Christ spirit slowly approached humanity, in anticipation of His mission, from out of the spiritual Sun Sphere and worked directly through heralds including the Archangel Michael who, in the ancient Greek world, was recognized as Apollo. In ancient Persia, Michael was recognized as "Marduk". During the Persian period, the Christ worked through the great initiate Zarathustra, or Zoroaster, who founded the Zoroastrian religion and is remembered today as a mighty Persian prophet. This man, the greatest of initiates, was known as the Sun-Initiate. He was the forerunner and prior incarnation of the man who later incarnated as Jesus and was transformed after Golgotha into the greatest leader of humanity; Christ-Jesus.

Over time, Steiner revealed that the Christ brings His profound transformative influences into the world eternally and over time. His forces were not introduced all at once during the crucifixion, but rather work within human beings gradually over time as each individual matures. Dr. Steiner reveals that the earth's aura now resonates with the Christ's forces and has been forever changed. Human beings as individuals approach this reality, and the revelation of His being, across the world at varying degrees of transformation. Thus, each of us is approaching the Christ based on our choices, dispositions, karma, and destiny. Each moment, His forces grow with intensity within the human being. Christ-Jesus is supported by a vast array of mighty beings and the great leaders of humanity, as high initiates and masters who are supported by coworkers who serve Him, who bring His impulse into the world throughout epochs of time. This includes Joan of Arc who acted directly on behalf of the Christ and the guidance of the Archangel Michael for a special mission at a crisis point in history.[72]

---

[72] Refer to the works of Rudolf Steiner, including Christianity as a Mystical Fact, for an expanded study of the Christ and how His influences are brought to humanity over time. Steiner refers to the Christ as a higher being of the Sun (and Light) who came into the

Chapter 2: Historical State of Affairs in the 15th Century

"Edward III with the Black Prince after the Battle of Crécy", 1788, by Benjamin West (1738-1820).

The historical events that led up to the crisis that occurred during the period of Joan of Arc are numerous and extend far back into history. For the sake of this study, perhaps, it is sufficient to provide a brief overview of some of the sources of the exoteric historical influences from the 8th century on. It is clear from a historical study that forces, and influences, were being thrust upon each other as Western Europe took form after the fall of the Roman Empire. The leading impulse in Europe in the Middle Ages occurred through Charlemagne (742-814AD) who thrust back the Saracens, albeit not in their entirety, and through his grandsons gave birth to the spirit and form of modern France and Germany. Over time, France became a competing series of Duchies that came into conflict with another. In England, the Anglo-Saxons through Alfred the Great (849-899AD) came into conflict with the Danes, Scots, and Picts as they sought, through Alfred's descendants, to unite England under one common leader. This unification was successful, for a time, under Aethelstan who defeated the Danes and the Scots at the Battle of Brunanburh in 937AD in a historic victory that

---

physical world and merged with the man Jesus. After Golgotha, Dr. Steiner refers to Him as "Christ-Jesus" who, having shed his blood for the world, merged with it for all time. Dr. Steiner provides deep insights into how this occurred and the spiritual facts of the event.

had, up to that point, not been achieved anywhere else against the Vikings. Thus, Aethelstan became the first "king" of England although there was no official title as such at that time.[73] It is a fact that British imperialism, as a unified stream in Britain, began during this period and blossomed later in a variety of ways.

So, the first modern construct of England began to take shape in an imperialistic way supported by a strong international policy that facilitated infrastructure, church building, and trade between England and Europe in a more structured manner. This was expanded through intermarriage with European countries including Germany and France. Thus, through Alfred the Great's and Charlemagne's descendants, intermarriages occurred throughout the Danish kingdoms, France, and Germanic areas. During that period of the 8th century forward, the spiritual-cultural impulses for the two modern nations were shaped out of the bloodlines of people who blended in unique ways and modern Europe began to take form. It was this blending, through the royal bloodlines, that brought England and France into a struggle for dominance in the Hundred Years War.

This struggle is exemplified, perhaps, in the lifetimes of leaders such as Charlemagne, Alfred the Great, William the Conqueror (1027-1087) and the Norman conquests of England, Henry II (1183-1199) and his descendants such as Richard the Lionhearted (1157-1199) who attempted to reign England from abroad (from Normandy and also while leading the 3rd crusade in Palestine) and thus further blend the two developing nations into one.[74] The historical study behind all of the leaders and their descendants is important and interesting, to say the least, but it is not critical for addressing the significance of Joan of Arc's mission. What is important to consider is that many individuals brought forth impulses in certain ways, as led by their unique destinies, through French and English cultural spiritual influences that eventually came into conflict with one another.[75]

---

[73] The prefix "Aethel" was a royal term that applied to members of the Anglo-Saxon royal bloodlines that originated in Mercia and Wessex in the 9th centuries.

[74] France was a disparate group of Duchies prior to the 15th century. During William and Richard's time, uprising occurred and efforts were always made to suppress and unite the aspects of both nations under one leader.

[75] For example, the Plantagenet banner was created under Henry II for the first time and the three primary English houses of York, Lancaster, and Beaufort were born. These three houses came into conflict with another during the Wars of the Roses as they struggled for power. The herald of the Plantagenet Lion was created during Henry II's reign and the first

Thus, the French crisis of the 15th century is the culmination of the Hundred Years' War truly began much further back in time but gained momentum in the year 1346 at the Battle of Crécy as led by Edward III and his first son, Edward the "Black Prince". In political terms, the sequence of events of the Hundred Years' War is fairly simple to comprehend. The historical basis behind it and dates. are traceable. The intent of this overview is to provide background into the political environment of the events leading up to Joan's life. It is not the intent to exhaust and consider all of the historical nuances and details. This chapter is therefore by no means comprehensive and serves only to provide a historical basis by which the spiritual crisis of the 15th century manifested and shall be discussed in the next chapter.

The activities of that period were driven by royalty and the relationships within the royal bloodlines that were intermingled between England and France. The goals and activities of kings throughout the world in the Middle Ages and the medieval period were based on several factors including genealogy, inheritances, rights, wealth accumulation, and, as to be expected, egotism. Each king that followed in the footsteps of his father, or the path by which he came to power, had his (or her) own ideas on how things should be done. As a result, just like today, certain influences were exacerbated while others faded. This is the nature of the world we live in.

The war between France and England began when King Edward III decided to press his rights as King of France in 1346. This ongoing dispute was a part of the early activities of both countries that shared a common ancestry that began much earlier in time. The assertion of his rights over the French was achieved with a decisive victory over the French at the Battle of Crécy where some 15-20,000 French engaged an estimated English force of some 4,000 cavalry and foot-soldiers and 10,000 archers. Despite heavy losses, the French continued to assault the English lines and were cut down by archers. The French may have lost as much as 40-50% of their forces compared to the English where varying estimates agree that the losses were minimal (some estimates are less than 1%). It was a tremendous one-sided victory and, in reality, reflects the incompetence of French military

---

evidence we see of it is on Richard I's official royal seal. My research suggests, however, that the first true blended French-English herald occurred, in fact, under Richard I (Fleur De Lys and Plantagenet Lion) although the first hard historical evident of this royal English heraldic does not appear until the reign of Edward III.

leadership. From that point forward, a series of battles, political changes, agreements, and rivalries took place over the next several decades. During this period, political instability in England led to the usurpation of King Richard II by a certain Henry Bolingbroke in 1399 who became King Henry IV. Thus, Henry's bloodline, although linked to Edward III, took precedence over those descended through Richard II.[76] Henry IV eventually died in 1413 leaving his reign to his son, Henry V.

Meanwhile, France was passing through growth pains and challenges as well at the royal level. King Charles VI, known as the "Mad King", was King of France from 1380 until his death in 1422. He is remembered historically for some form of mental illness and psychotic episodes that plagued him throughout his life. In 1422, he was replaced by his son, Henry VII, who brought his weaknesses and lack of leadership with him that led to a severe and pivotal crisis point in French, English, and world history. France, who had a history of strong and inspired leadership including men such as Charles Martel "The Hammer", Charlemagne, and Louis IX the Pious was descending to a crisis point. For whatever reason, France's political leadership took a turn for the worse with the reign of Charles VI and this curse, as it were, of uninspired and weak-willed leadership followed his son.

So, during the period in which Joan lived, Henry V, as the son of Henry IV, claimed the title of King of France through his great-grandfather Edward III of England, although in practice the English kings were generally prepared to renounce this claim if the French would acknowledge the English claim on the region of Aquitaine and other French lands.[77] Henry called for a "Great Council" in the spring of 1414 to discuss war with France, but the English lords that surrounded him insisted that he should negotiate further and moderate his claims before any military action. In the ensuing negotiations with France, Henry V agreed that he give up his claim to the French throne if, and only if, the French agreed to pay him the vast sum of 1,600,000 crowns that were due to England from a ransom demand of John II who had been captured at the Battle of Poitiers in 1356 and further concede the lands of Anjou, Brittany, Flanders, Normandy, Touraine, and Aquitaine to England. Henry proposed to marry Catherine, the young

---

[76] This is only important because this division eventually led to a civil war and crisis in England after Joan's death that is referred today as the "Wars of the Roses".

[77] This agreement was made under the terms of the Treaty of Brétigny in 1360.

daughter of Charles VI, and receive a dowry of the vast sum of 2,000,000 crowns.[78]

In 15th century terms, this was a massive sum of money. Surely this demand would have bankrupted the French treasury. The French responded as they did not want war with England, with terms of marriage to the French Princess Catherine, a dowry of 600,000 crowns, and the enlarged region of Aquitaine. Insulted, Henry disagreed and claimed that the French had mocked his claims and shirked him as the rightful King of England and France.[79] Negotiations came to a halt. In December of 1414, Henry took a "request" to the English parliament to grant Henry a double tax subsidy, that in essence was a tax of twice the traditional rate on English landowners. As parliament consisted of men who owned royal lands, they would bear the burden of the French's obligations unless they agreed to war with France, which they were reluctant to do. Henry argued this was the only way for him to recover his rightful inheritance that was due him by the French.[80] If he could not acquire his repatriations through the French, he would get it through the English nobility! This genuine threat to the wealth and property of the English aristocracy paid off. On April 19, 1415, parliament agreed to war with France.

King Henry V invaded France on August 12, 1415. His forces besieged a fortress at Harfleur capturing it on September 22. Henry then marched with his army across the French countryside toward Calais despite the warnings of his council and won a pivotal battle against the French at the Battle of Agincourt. The French held the advantage in terms of numbers, so the victory was unexpected. This defeat of the French army boosted English morale and prestige, crippled France, and started a new period of English dominance. In tactical terms, the Battle of Agincourt was an archer's victory due to the English and Welsch longbowman and the fact that the French infantry and cavalry were severely impeded by the terrain and the heavy rainfall the night before. The French lacked the power and range of the English longbowman. It was a strange twist of fate as the

---

[78] It was rumored that Charles VI suffered from bouts of genuine mental illness, thus he is remembered historically as "the Mad King" or "Charles the Mad".

[79] Thus, we see the manifestation of egotism that led to apex of the crisis.

[80] The practice of taxing the Dukes and Earls who were landowners was a standard method of collecting revenues in England during that period. All Dukes, and wealthy landowners, were appointed by the King and secured their futures only through the King. In turn, they paid the royal treasury a tax, or tithe, that was due at certain points of the calendar year.

English were, at that time, trying to withdraw from France after Henry V's army had dwindled in numbers due to starvation and disease. The deportation point was by way of Calais, a primary port at that time, but was cut off by the French army. It is estimated that Henry V's losses were only 10% of the French.

Thus, an intensification of the English occupation of France began. The invasion of France began in earnest in 1417. Caen fell. Rouen was taken in 1419 after a six-month siege where half of the population died of starvation and disease. Leading French nobles were punished and executed. After Henry V died in 1422, the power passed to his brother, John of Lancaster Duke of Bedford who shared Henry's intelligence, will, and zeal for the continuation of English claims on the French crown. Thus, a series of battles and skirmishes followed over the course of the next ten years and continued for some time after Joan's death in 1431. The English-held territory was divided amongst Henry's Dukes who held absolute authority over the English and French alike. Although Henry V allegedly discouraged looting and pillaging by soldiers and knights, he was unable to prevent these activities from occurring and as a result, widespread raiding parties, looting, and crimes against French peasants continued for the next decade. France became a disease and poverty-stricken war-torn country. The neighbors of France, the Burgundians, watched these events unfold and took advantage of the situation by invading the neighboring areas of France and claiming it for themselves.

Thus, due to Henry V's invasion and military successes, France was essentially divided into separate spheres of political, economic, and cultural autonomy. It was the intent of England, and Burgundy, to conquer and submit the French to their authority and not to be simple passive governors. France was being transformed into an English and Burgundian country.

The theft of food, livestock, assaults and the kidnapping of women, and the burning and destruction of property were commonplace during that difficult time. Joan of Arc's village of Domrémy was allegedly burned at least once.[81] In some areas, the French nobility followed the same path and behavior as the English as they were suffering from starvation and disease. The threat of the bubonic plague was still in existence in the 1420s and impacted about half of France's population in the mid-14th century. So, it

---

[81] Per testimony from the retrial of 1452-1456.

was not uncommon for French nobility or the captains that held French garrisons, to appear randomly and confiscate livestock and property from the French peasantry. Mercenaries also raided the countryside at will. The English became known to the French peasantry in many areas as "black knights".

In some towns and cities, such as Paris, the mayors lost faith and trust in the French government due to the scheming of Charges VI and his son Charles VII. By the time of Charles VII's reign, many of the cities refused to cooperate with the French leadership having been betrayed once too often as Charles VI and VII frequently bartered and traded towns and villages through secret agreements and parlays as though these communities of people were nothing more than pawns on a chessboard. Large towns, such as Rouen and Paris, were fortified with high defensive walls and sometimes moats that could only be breached by an extended siege thus the mayors of those towns held considerable influence and defensive capabilities. Paris was the strongest fortified city in the region and fell under English and Burgundian influence until about 1437 when Charles VII entered the city unopposed thanks to Joan's efforts.

No one was safe. The country was divided and towns and villages turned against one another as loyalties and financial interests determined each person's allegiance. Refugees and transients appeared across the landscape, driven from their homes by English and Burgundian raiding parties who often burned homes and killed livestock. The plague was rampant. In each village, loyalties were divided and people spied on one another. Across the French landscape, the behavior and disposition of the English, French, and Burgundian nobility varied but on average most were inherently cruel to the peasantry who bore the burden of that time of chaos and transformation. It was a time of exploitation and a struggle for survival for the French peoples...

In this malaise of tension, stress, poverty, terror, and crisis, the French were worn down by one embittered defeat after another that gained momentum with the Battle of Agincourt in 1415. France became a nation of each man for himself, as it were, and the French no longer considered themselves "French" at all. They had become citizens of villages and cities who allied or turned against one another having suffered under the yoke of English, French, or Burgundian tyranny. Blackmail was common and bribes were paid by villages to noble lords to escape the looting and pillaging by ruffians; English, Burgundian, and French alike. The French lost the will to fight in a unified way due to distrust, exhaustion, poverty, illness, and desperation.

By 1428, King Charles VII had retreated to a stronghold at the small yet well-fortified town of Chinon. The gateway to this royal citadel, as it were, was through the fortified town of Orléans. If Orléans fell, the English army would easily push through the area into France and capture the king. As Orléans fell under siege by the English, and defeat was imminent, the Maid of Lorraine appeared as guided, and driven, by the forces of providence and divine spiritual beings. The reality of Joan's involvement is, in fact, not a political illusion or invention of a myth to rally the people. Joan's mission was a genuine spiritual and cultural task and fulfillment. Unbeknownst to most people at that time, France possessed a unique role to play in the destiny of the world and it was not her fate, or the will of the beings who oversee humanity's development, to be absorbed into England and Burgundy.

However, behind these political events were spiritual influences. Much more was occurring at the global level than just the political issues of France and her struggles with England and Burgundy. The activities of people are, in fact, the result of the activities of spiritual beings. Unbeknownst to the masses, the future construct of Europe, and the world, was at stake as a change in consciousness was due to be introduced into humanity as a new impulse from the spiritual worlds. This impulse would lead humanity one step closer to spiritual freedom and the Christ. This spiritual task was connected to the cultural, and therefore national, construct of Europe.

Therefore, as the English forces pressed further into France, the imperialistic cultural impulse of the English threatened all of Europe. As each country possesses its own cultural identity, impulse, and influence as guided and directed by the Folk Spirits who reside in the spiritual worlds, this threat had to be neutralized so that Europe, and humanity, could progress appropriately.

Chapter 3: The 15th Century in Light of Spiritual Science

According to Dr. Steiner, Joan's mission and task carried a far deeper significance than what can be perceived through any intellectual review. The outcome of her mission superseded that of a common farm-woman who could neither read nor write and was guided by the forces of destiny with the purely regional task of the political liberation of the French peoples. While the circumstances of Joan's accomplishment from a historical point of view is a clear indication that something unique and special occurred in and of itself, the true spiritual causes and outcomes of her accomplishments are not confined to the political and social consequences of France. They were intertwined at that moment in time. Joan's mission worked in that area with the task to support a destined global change that was being brought forth by the spiritual hierarchies.

As discussed in Chapter 1, based on the research of Dr. Steiner, over time the Spiritual Hierarchies introduce transformations and changes into humanity. In that regard, Joan of Arc came into the world on a specific mission that would enable the introduction of a new spiritual element of the human being. This new aspect of the human soul is referred to as the "Consciousness Soul" by Dr. Steiner. This new faculty, or aspect of human consciousness, was released into humanity from the spiritual worlds in the 15th century. Joan's role was connected to this task, which had global significance, through her deeds thus enabled by the Christ to work within her being in a tangible and living way. Her task was simply to lead the French to push the English out of Europe. This was central to the fulfillment of this impulse in the future as it came to work through the nations of Europe. Thus, Joan helped to ensure that this necessary shift that was destined to occur came into reality.

Steiner points to the year 1413AD, just one year after Joan's birth, as the key date for this change. However, he also indicates that it was a gradual change that began to take form within humanity before that year and gradually unfolded over time. This date also represents the beginning of a new epoch of transformation for humanity that began in 747BC with the founding of Rome that ended in 1413AD. Steiner further states that this change has expanded throughout the world over time as a gradual shift that has come into full expression in the 19th and 20th centuries. He describes this change as "the last great revolution in men's consciousness that took place in the 15th century."[82]

Reviewing all of the nuances of this change is outside the scope of this study, and the author's capabilities, thus I attempt only to provide a few comments on the nature of this faculty as described by Dr. Steiner. I recommend turning to Steiner's body of knowledge to explore this element and the implications of all that this change in consciousness represents. Given its direct correlation to Joan's mission, it is clearly important to consider it in this study.[83]

> "The last great incision into the historical evolution of mankind is the one that took place...in the first third of the 15th century, and that marks the transition from the evolution more particularly of the Intellectual or Mind-Soul to that of the Consciousness or Spiritual Soul."[84]

Steiner describes the *Consciousness Soul* as a member, or aspect, of the human being that is related to the spirit and the capability of independent reflection. It is the one aspect of our being that enables us the potential of having self-consciousness and thus full awareness of ourselves as individuals in relation to the human spirit. Human beings have always possessed consciousness, so this term does not suggest that people before this period were unconscious. It is a change within the soul aspect of the human being that has shaped us into individuals capable of true independent thought and self-consciousness. It is an inner spiritual faculty, or change in consciousness, and not an intellectual attribute. Many of the people before the 15th century possessed razor-sharp intellects including the interrogators at the trial of Joan of Arc as the records reveal. The capacity for true "independent reflection...came only with the development of the Consciousness Soul."[85]

The individual who experiences the effects of the Consciousness Soul rebels against constructs that disallow one to think for one's self and arrive at an independent judgment. For example, Steiner reveals several examples in the 15th century of individuals who were striving to arrive at an

---

[82] Steiner, Rudolf. World History in Light of Anthroposophy, Lecture VII, December 30, 1923.

[83] Steiner, Rudolf. From Symptom to Reality in Modern History, Lecture 1.

[84] Steiner, Rudolf. World History in the light of Anthroposophy.

[85] Steiner, Rudolf. From Symptom to Reality in Modern History, Lecture 1.

independent judgment of ideas, thoughts, and observations on their own against the influences of the Catholic Church which exerted a heavy suggestive influence on the nations and individuals of Europe before the 15th century. It is because of the influences of the Consciousness Soul that humanity began to break away from the autonomy of the Church.

> "...let us now turn to the more inward happenings which are related more to the impulse of the Consciousness Soul which is breaking through the shell of the human soul. Let us consider, for example, the Council of Constance and the burning of Hus. In Hus we see a personality who stands out, so to speak, like a human volcano. The Council of Constance which passed sentence on him opened in 1414, in the early years of the fifteenth century which marked the birth of the Consciousness Soul. Now in the annals of modern history Hus stands out as a symbol of protest against the suggestionism of the universalist impulse of Catholicism. In Jan Hus the Consciousness Soul itself rebels against all that the Rational or Intellectual soul had received from this universalist Catholic impulse.

> "And this was not an isolated phenomenon — we could show how this ground had already been prepared by the struggle of the Albigenses against Catholic domination. In Savonarola in Italy and in others we see the revolt of the autonomous personality who wishes to arrive at his religious faith by relying upon his own judgment and rejects the suggestionism of papal Catholicism. And this same spirit of independence persists in Luther, in the emancipation of the Anglican Church from Rome..."[86]

> "The dawning of the Consciousness Soul signifies a new relationship to these (existing) problems but does not herald the birth of new impulses."[87]

Thus, this aspect represents an impulse for self-consciousness and full conscious independence in a spiritual and individual way. It casts things in a new light through independent judgment. This new aspect of the human spirit inspired countless changes throughout the world over the coming centuries. The battleground for this change, in physical and outer terms, occurred throughout Europe but the separation of England and France, at

---

[86] Ibid.

[87] Steiner, Rudolf. From Symptom to Reality in Modern History, Lecture 1.

the national and cultural level, represents the critical point by which this transformation would be successful in the future.

> "Whilst for centuries these countries (England and France) had shared a common purpose, differences began to emerge in the fifteenth century. The first indications are seen in the appearance of Joan of Arc in 1429, a most important turning point in modern history. It was this appearance of Joan of Arc which gave the impetus...which led to the differentiation between the French and the English character. Thus, we see the emergence of nationalism as the architect of the community and at the same time this differentiation which is so significant for the evolution of modern mankind."[88]

When new impulses are introduced into humanity by the Spiritual Hierarchies who oversee human progress and transformation, they are always met with opposition. Steiner reveals that the Luciferic and Ahrimanic forces are always at work and as a result, conflicts and contradictions often arise.

> "When a phenomenon of this nature emerges on the surface it meets with counter-pressure from the past. The normal course of evolution, as you know, is always accompanied by Luciferic and Ahrimanic forces which derive from backward impulses and seek to assert themselves. Every normal impulse entering into mankind must fight against the subtle invasion of Luciferic and Ahrimanic forces. Thus, the impulse that was clearly manifest in Hus, Luther, Calvin and Wyclif had to battle with these forces. A symptom of this struggle is seen in the revolt of the United Netherlands and in the Luciferic-Ahrimanic personality of Philip of Spain."[89]

It is hard to fathom in dogmatic terms, but the birth of modern forms of nationalism,[90] gained momentum in the 15th century due to the introduction of this new spiritual attribute which had, up to that time, existed in either a dormant form or was lacking from the human being. One

---

[88] Steiner, Rudolf. From Symptom to Reality, Lecture 1.

[89] Ibid.

[90] Steiner reveals that nationalism obviously always exited in the human construct, but that it took on a new form and character at this moment in time. This impulse was supported by the innovation of a Parliament which took root at that time.

result of this change was that it brought an end to the overarching influence of the Papacy on the nations of Europe.

> "Thus, we see the emergence of nationalism as the architect of the community and at the same time this differentiation which is so significant for the evolution of modern mankind. This turning point is marked by the appearance of Joan of Arc in 1429. At the moment when the impulse of the Papacy is compelled to release from its clutches the population of Western Europe, at that moment the consciousness of nationality gathers momentum in the West and shapes its future."[91]

As Steiner reveals, Joan's mission was directly tied to the destiny of nations as carriers of spiritual-cultural streams of activity that flowed through into human beings out of the spiritual worlds and thus impacted all of humanity. Each unique cultural impulse, as brought forth by Folk Spirits, is unique and possesses a rightful place in the world and therefore has a peculiar destiny that interpolates one another in a myriad of ways. The cultures of the world influence one another in unique ways at any given moment in time and, just like individuals, transform and evolve.

> "When we trace back the history of Europe to the event connected with the personality of the Maid of Orléans we must say, even if we only consider the external course of history: What the Maid of Orléans did, when she rose up from the heart of the French nation and vanquished the English forces — for she actually achieved this — really implied that the map of Europe took on the aspect which it afterwards gradually assumed. Any other concept of history relating to the past centuries, in so far as it refers to the European distribution of nations and states, is an invention that does not take into account the fact that the Christ-Impulse lived in the Maid of Orléans that a living Impulse brought about the distribution of the European nations and national forces."[92]

Another aspect of the introduction of the Consciousness Soul into humanity was that it inspired the English people, and indeed all of Europe, towards a parliamentary government. This move towards parliament was a

---

[91] Ibid.

[92] Steiner, Rudolf. Spiritual Science, a Necessity for the Present Time. Nuremberg, March 13, 1915.

byproduct of the English Civil War, or the Wars of the Roses, in England (1452-1485). The Wars of the Roses took place only after England was pushed out of France by the efforts of Joan of Arc. When that occurred, England's cultural imperialistic forces turned within and she, like France, also reached a crisis point. It was a time of strife and transformation, yet Steiner reveals that certain developments occurred by way of Joan's efforts that began to resonate throughout the world.

"Now it is a remarkable and significant phenomenon that after the separate development of France and England, there emerged in England at this time, after slow and careful preparation, that which later became the system of parliamentary government in Europe. As a result of the long civil wars which lasted from 1452–1480 (the English Civil Wars), we see developing, amongst manifold external symptoms, the historical symptom of embryonic parliamentary government. When the era of the Consciousness Soul opened in the early fifteenth century people wanted to take their affairs into their own hands.

"They wanted to debate, to discuss, to have a say in future policies and to shape external events accordingly — or at least liked to imagine that they shaped events. This spirit of independence — as a result of the disastrous civil wars in the fifteenth century — developed in England out of that configuration which was markedly different from what had also arisen in France under the influence of the national impulse. Parliamentary Government in England developed out of the national impulse.

"We must clearly recognize that, through the birth of parliamentary government as a consequence of the English civil wars in the fifteenth century, we see the interplay, or, if you like, the interpenetration, the interfusion of the emergent national idea on the one hand, and on the other hand an impulse clearly orientated towards that which the Consciousness Soul seeks to realize...it is precisely because of these events that the impulse of the Consciousness Soul breaks through in England and assumes the character of that national impulse..."[93]

---

[93] Steiner, Rudolf. From Symptom to Reality in Modern History. Lecture 1.

Steiner also reveals that England was dominating France through a cultural impulse that consisted predominantly of Anglo-Saxon influences. The French, on the other hand, were more heavily influenced by cultural forces that were Norman-Roman in origin.[94] The French represented a certain aristocratic aspect while the Anglo-Saxons represented a lower and, perhaps, expansionary and domineering aspect. While both nations possessed some measure of Roman-Norman influences, the cultural imperialism of the Anglo-Saxons was prevalent and pushed into France. Steiner reveals that the French, at that moment in time, were of a distinctly different spiritual-cultural disposition compared to the English.

> "At that time there was a complete separation between the French nature and the British nature. This British being originally arose from the Angles and Saxons... Now, at the time of Joan of Arc, this Anglo-Saxon layer was ruled by the Norman-Roman element and formed a lower caste. That particular British beingness which today is the superior, only happened since the 17th century, at the time when the French element was still working, and the Anglo-Saxons were the lower layer and the French spirit was the aristocratic spirit. They despised everything coming from the Angles and Saxons... You were not supposed to be an Englander if you wanted to be well regarded. However, this changed fundamentally after the separation occurred through Joan of Arc..."[95]

Steiner reveals that a prevailing Luciferic impulse was dominant during the 15th century. It was because of this polarized influence, that the soul who became Joan was selected by the guiding beings of humanity as she had overcome Luciferic influences in her soul-being and thus could effectively serve a broader purpose on behalf of the higher beings who oversee humanity's transformation.[96]

---

[94] As history reveals, Rome invaded Britannia under Julius Caesar in about 55BC and Roman cultural influences were imbued into England's destiny including imperialism, militarism, and legalism. Rome, through Caesar and those that followed him, also invaded Gaul thus bringing certain Graeco-Roman cultural influences into the cultural origins of what became the French, German, and European nations. This impulse also had an effect on the various tribes in those areas including the Anglo-Saxon peoples, who would become the founders of the English culture as they blended with the Nordic and Celtic peoples.

[95] Steiner, Rudolf. From Symptom to Modern Reality, Lecture 1.

[96] For those who are familiar with the trials and tribulations of human spiritual transformation, even in a nascent way, this is a significant and major spiritual

"What was the mission of Joan of Arc, really, if we consider something that was present throughout her whole life? She was taken hold of from within by the forces of the divine spiritual world. In her soul these forces encountered the Luciferic forces. These Luciferic forces were mighty and powerful at that time. Joan of Arc bore something within her that made her vanquish the Luciferic forces."[97]

"This was a time when the spiritual forces, seeking to evolve man according to the potentialities laid in him from the very beginning by yet loftier Divine-Spiritual Powers, encountered their strong adversaries. These adversaries wish to divert man into channels other than those appointed for him from the beginning. If they were to succeed, man would not be able to apply the forces of his origin to his further evolution...It would become a dying, withering part within his being. The consequence would be that man could then fall a prey to the Luciferic or Ahrimanic Powers and lose his own true and proper development. If the adversaries of mankind had succeeded in their efforts — if they had not only put hindrances in the way, but achieved complete success — the entry of the Spiritual (Consciousness) Soul could have been prevented."[98]

This fact is evidenced repeatedly in Joan's behavior when she refused the temptations associated with someone who was playing the role that she was asked to take on. Like the Christ who entered Jerusalem on a donkey, and not a great white horse, Joan rejected all forms of Luciferic forces as they manifested themselves on her journey. Sometimes, as always, Luciferic temptations can be encountered in subtle and seemingly innocuous forms. She did not punish her enemies, refused vindictiveness, and abhorred forms of egotism and self-aggrandizement. For example:

---

accomplishment and because of this, Joan was a true spiritual leader at that moment in history and thus able to fulfill a broader mission on behalf of humanity.

[97] Steiner, Rudolf. The Destinies of Individuals and of Nations, Lecture 5. The Nature of the Christ Impulse and the Michaelic Sprit Serving It.

[98] Steiner, Rudolf. Anthroposophical Leading Thoughts. Second Study: How the Michael Forces Work in the Earliest Unfolding of the Spiritual Soul. For a deeper understanding of the meaning of the "spiritual soul" and its significance consult the lectures and works of Rudolf Steiner. This turning point in time represents a change in consciousness for humanity as brought forth by the spiritual hierarchies.

"She was good not only to the French, but also to the enemy. All this I know of a surety, for I was for a long time with her, and many times assisted in arming her. Jeanne lamented much, and was displeased when certain good women came to her, wishing to salute her: it seemed to her like adoration, at which she was angered."[99]

Here, even though she possesses unique spiritual faculties that most others lack, and she knows that she is in direct communication with angelic guides who are guiding her on a divine mission, Joan openly rejects the temptation to be considered as one who possesses some divine saintly aspect:

"I remember that many women came to my house while Jeanne was living there, and brought paternosters and other religious objects that she might touch them; but Jeanne laughed, saying: "Touch them yourselves. Your touch will do them as much good as mine."[100]

Succumbing to these flattering false notions would have opened Joan up to the vices of pride, egotism, and self-adoration. Having purged those impulses from her soul, she was, therefore, an ideal candidate, in karmic-spiritual terms, to undertake and fulfill a mission on behalf of the Christ at a moment in history when Luciferic forces were prevalent. In addition, as Joan recognized, she was not the actual bringer of a new impulse from the spiritual worlds into France and the world. That is the task of the Arch Angels/Folk Spirits and the Spiritual Hierarchies. Rather, Joan was following the orders of her angelic guides and in doing so became an effective vehicle by which the Christ and Michael could bring a fresh and forward impulse into humanity by ensuring that a certain outcome was achieved. She served a purpose as a bridge, and messenger, between the divine and the physical world.

"You also know from ordinary history that it was she who, under the unceasing impulse and urge of her intense faith — it would be better to say, through her actual vision — and in face of the greatest difficulties, led the armies to victory and the King to his crowning

---

[99] The English translation of the trial files from 1902. From the book: Jeanne d'Arc Maid of Orléans Deliverer of France. Edited by T. Douglas Murray, Deposition of Squire Simon Baucroix.
[100] Ibid. Deposition of Dame Marguerite La Touroulde widow of the late Réné de Bouligny, Councillor to the King.

(Charles VII). Who intervened at that time in the course of history? — None other than Beings of higher Hierarchies! The Maid of Orléans was an outer Instrument of these Beings, and it was they who guided the deeds of history."[101]

Joan's link as a counterforce to the Luciferic forces at that moment in time is further supported by the fact that, in terms of cosmic cycles, her lifetime was a spiritual fulfillment that can be traced back to the foundation of Rome (start of the Graeco-Roman period). This impulse carried several impulses including an imperialistic influence that came to manifest later on in England and France in a variety of ways including Rome. Joan of Arc's birth year of 1412[102] occurred exactly 2,160 years after the foundation of Rome in about 747BC.[103]

"We know that everything in the world goes in cycles, that things happen in such a way that important events come up in definite cycles. If we take the year of Joan's birth, 1412, we can ask a specific question relating to this. We are able to say that the year this Maid of Orléans was born the sun would of course have been in a particular position, astronomical position, coinciding with one of the constellations in the zodiac. The progress of the sun from one sign of the zodiac to the next marks a major time interval. Passing right through the zodiac the sun will go through all twelve constellations; the time interval needed for the sun to progress from one constellation in the zodiac to the next is approximately 2,160 years...Going back approximately 2,160 years from the birth of Joan of Arc we come to the founding of Rome."[104]

---

[101] Steiner, Rudolf. Occult History, Lecture 2. Stuttgart, 28th December 1910. The parenthesis is the author's.

[102] This coincides with Steiner's description of the 4th Post-Atlantean Epoch that ended in 1412. The introduction of the "Consciousness Soul" occurs precisely at the beginning of the 5th Post-Atlantean Epoch. Refer to Steiner's descriptions of the cultural epochs for more information.

[103] As elaborated upon in Chapter 1, 2,160 years is the period of time that represents one full "house" of the zodiac and a completion of one full rotation of the seven Archangels who rule in successive regencies of 300-400 years.

[104] Steiner, Rudolf. The Destinies of Individuals and Nations. Lecture 5, The Nature of the Christ Impulse and the Michaelic Sprit Serving It, Berlin, January 19, 1915. (1412AD – 2,160 years = 748AD).

In the case of France and England (and several other countries), Steiner provides further insights into the differentiation that occurred as a result of the changes that were brought about as a direct result of the introduction of the Consciousness Soul and Joan of Arc's intervention.[105] Many distinctions arose as a result of the two countries unique, and yet similar, cultural attributes that have a common ancestry that manifested in either nation's peculiar identity.

This reality probably explains why so many renowned artists and musicians came into being throughout and beyond the borders of France. England was not known at that moment in time for growing talented artists and musicians who primarily emerged out of areas throughout Germany, France, Switzerland, and Italy during and after the Renaissance period. Thus, it seems reasonable to infer that the flower of the Renaissance was heavily influenced by the efforts of Joan of Arc when England was pushed out of Europe. It seems self-evident based on the facts given to us by Dr. Steiner that had England achieved victory over the French, they would have pushed further into Europe thus dominating other nations and cultural impulses. The Renaissance would have taken on an entirely different character or been suppressed altogether. The countless ways that the cultures of Europe brought forth the creativity of the human spirit within spiritual movements, philosophers, artists, scientists, and musicians is incalculable.

> "What would the development of modern Europe have been if at the beginning of the 15th century the Maid of Orléans had not entered the arena of events? Anyone who thinks, even from an entirely external point of view, of the development that took place during this period, must say to himself: Suppose the deeds of the Maid of Orléans were erased from history ... then, according to the knowledge obtainable from purely external historical research, one cannot but realise that without the working of higher, super-sensible Powers through the Maid of Orléans, the whole of France, indeed the whole of Europe in the 15th century, would have taken on an altogether different form. Everything in the impulses of will, in the physical brains of those times, was directed towards flooding all Europe with a general conception of the State which would have extinguished the folk-individualities and under this influence a very great deal of what has developed in Europe during the last centuries

---

[105] Refer to Rudolf Steiner's lecture cycle From Symptom to Reality in Modern History.

through the interplay of these folk-individualities would quite certainly have been impossible."[106]

The opposing influences, as described in Chapter 1, play upon all of the activities of human relationships and continually attempt to thwart the progress of humanity as led by higher divine beings. During the period of Joan's life, Steiner reveals that Luciferic forces were prevalent while today Ahrimanic influences are dominant. Joan, due to the qualities of her being, effectively conquered the Luciferic forces at that time. Today, due to the conditions of the age in which we live, this would not be possible.

"Someone with a disposition like that of Joan of Arc would not be able to achieve anything in our day and age. She would be an interesting personality and would be able to reveal many marvelous things through prophecy and in other ways. Such a person capable of making intimate revelations is capable of effectively countering Luciferic forces. Today, however, man has to resist Ahrimanic forces, has to make himself strong to cope with these forces, developing the strength required in the Michaelic age. Sun-like qualities are called for in the age of Michael, qualities we take into ourselves by spiritualizing the powers we have at our command between waking up and going to sleep: the powers of the intellect, of understanding, of insight."[107]

So, in conclusion, spiritual-cultural influences brought forth through the nations of the world can come into conflict with one another based on karma, dispositions, and the interference of the opposing forces who continually try to impede humanity's progress. Such was the state of affairs that occurred in the 15th century. During that period, the opposing powers had influenced human beings in a certain way over long periods of time that led to a crisis. A differentiation of the English and French cultural streams needed to occur in order to set them back on the proper path of spiritual, and human, transformation. In this way, with England being pushed out of France, the *revolution in consciousness* could come into being to its fullest effect in the world. By Joan's actions, as guided by the Christ, the Archangel Michael, and the Spiritual Hierarchies, the changes

---

[106] Steiner, Rudolf. Occult History, Lecture 2. Stuttgart, December 28. 1910.
[107] Steiner, Rudolf. The Destinies of Individuals and Nations, Lecture 5
The Nature of the Christ Impulse and the Michaelic Sprit Serving It, January 19, 1915.

that were intended to come into the world could then blossom to their fullest effect thus transforming it forever.

"The marvelous thing happened that a poor shepherd girl from Orléans, Joan of Arc, did everything those who were very advanced for their time had not been able to do. At that time, it was indeed the Christ impulse acting in Joan of Arc, through its Michaelic servants, that prevented a possible merging of France and England, causing England to be forced back onto its island. And this achieved two things: first, France continued to have a free hand in Europe. This can be seen if we study the history of France over the following centuries — the essential element of the French spirit was able to influence European culture entirely without hindrance. The second thing which was achieved was that England was given its domain outside the continent of Europe. This deed, brought in through Joan of Arc, was a blessing not only for the French but also for the English, compelling them to take up their domain."[108]

"It was with this intention that reference was made among other historical events to Joan of Arc through whom this Christ impulse resolved a major issue in the 15th century through its servant, the Michaelic spirit, and for the good and advancement of mankind. The reason why it was particularly important to refer to this event was that in our day, too, it does hold true that everything destined to regulate events on the historical scale is ordered and regulated from the spiritual worlds. We need to be aware that the forces, the impulses, for what is to happen come to us from the spiritual worlds."[109]

---

[108] Steiner, Rudolf. The Destinies of Individuals and of Nations, Lecture 4, The Nature of the Christ Impulse and the Michaelic Sprit Serving It, Part 1.
[109] Ibid. Lecture 5. Part 2.

"Joan of Arc Listening to the Voices" by French artist Diogène Ulysse Napoléon Maillart (1840-1926). Joan revealed that the voices began when she was about 13 years of age in her father's garden (1424-1425AD). Joan revealed later that her voices were those of St. Michael, St. Gabriel, St. Margaret, and St. Catherine. Note, the artist portrays Joan as an Oracle in the Greek tradition as the visions of the Saints are emerging out of the smoke in the tradition of the Oracle of Delphi. While Joan did not follow this practice, this is a clear indication of the artist's intent to draw a correlation between Joan and the Oracles of ancient Greece.

"Priestess of Delphi" by John Collier, 1891.

A Sybil, in the context of the ancient world, was a prophetess who was born with an inherited form of clairvoyance and possessed the ability to act as a bridge between the divine and the people. This was accomplished through a spiritual link to nature and the elements. The Oracles were recognized as genuine intermediaries between the living, the dead, and the divine. Each shrine that the Oracles and the Sybils occupied in the ancient world was unique. Many scholars and historians have speculated on the nature of the Oracle's influences including nonsense. However, in reality, many of these seers were genuine. They were always women who maintained their virtue and were protected by law. They were recognized as genuine prophetesses who could provide valuable insights into the human soul, the future, and the world.

The Oracles, and Sybils, of ancient Greece were not slaves nor were they considered superstitious soothsayers to be mocked. These seers were treated with veneration and respect.[110] Patrons approached the shrines cautiously with reverence and courtesy. Oftentimes, the ancient Sybils spoke in riddles or stanzas, thus their messages were open to interpretation. The Oracle at Delphi was the most well-known and regarded Oracle in ancient Greece. Well-known leaders, such as Alexander the Great, consulted the Oracle of Delphi.

---

[110] Historically, the two terms of "Oracle" and "Sybil" are ambiguous and used interchangeably. The Oracles were renowned throughout Greece and the term Sybil seems to have been historically applied during the Roman era. However, the concept is the same.

A Sibyl, as described in Steiner's lectures, was a woman who employed a natural and inherited form of clairvoyance that was intimately connected to the environment, nature, and the hidden spiritual aspects and powers of the elements. In the modern world, the masses are not aware of these influences, thus in modern terms, the concept of a sibyl is illusory and superstitious. References to Sybils are made throughout ancient Greek writings and the sibyl was an accepted part of the Gallic, Nordic, and Druidic cultures although they were known by different names. Thus, to the ancient Greeks who were more consciously connected to the powers of the natural world, the power of the sibyls and Oracles manifested as a valid means of spiritual perception and communication. In art, the Sybils are portrayed in several ways, but valid portrayals connect them to the elements of nature. For example:

> "...Michelangelo places the Sibyls, who are open to the elemental powers of the Earth. Thus, the hair of one Sibyl is blown about by the wind; even her blue mantle billows in the wind, and under the influence of the wind she utters her prophecies. We see another Sibyl seized by inner fire; in the typically assertive gesture of her hand, we see the fire, the earthly element. We could look again at these Sibyls one by one and we should find that they live in the midst of the forces which play into their souls from the elemental surroundings of the Earth. These Sibylline forces, which so to speak draw into their souls the spirit of the elements and bring it to expression."[111]

Dr. Steiner reveals that Joan demonstrated the qualities of a 15th-century Sybil. However, Steiner also provided a perspective that the nature of Joan's individuality, as a seer with genuine inherited clairvoyant faculties, is more than that. She was also spiritually imbued with the impulse of the Christ in a spiritual event that occurred before Joan was born. As a result, Joan of Arc was described by Steiner as a "Christ-Filled Sibyl".[112]

A Sybil's spiritual faculty and power are intimately connected to the powers of the elements and nature. As communicated by Steiner, this phenomenon followed the remnants of the Greek culture into Europe but faded into the background after the Greek culture fell into decadence and

---

[111] Steiner, Rudolf. Christ and the Spiritual World: The Search for the Holy Grail, Lecture 4. December 31, 1913.
[112] Ibid. Lecture 6. January 2, 1914.

her cultural impulses spread out across the globe. These inherited clairvoyant abilities were transformed by way of the Christ event in 33AD. It was the Christ who, through the global impulse that He brought forth through his sacrifice on Golgotha, brought about a transformational impulse and purified the Sibylline forces within humanity.

> "When the Christ Impulse entered into the evolution of humanity in the way known to us, one result was that the chaotic forces of the Sibyls were thrust back for a time, as when a stream disappears below ground and reappears later on. These forces were indeed to reappear in another form, a form purified by the Christ Impulse, after the Christ Impulse had entered into the aura of the earth."[113]

Thus, Joan represents a reemergence of this clairvoyant capability in a refined and transformed way by the Christ. Steiner describes Joan not as a throwback to a prior time or one confined to the ancient traditions, as though she were lacking something that needed to be transformed, but rather as a genuine seer and bridge to the spiritual worlds who was permeated by the Christ that was transformed at that moment in time. Steiner describes Joan as one who bears the forces of the Christ, and the Archangel Michael, within her as a chosen representative and bearer of His spiritual forces that she brought into the world through her deeds.

> "...something like a modern Sibyl emerged in the Maid of Orléans. It was the time — the fifteenth century...a time when the Christ Impulse had to emerge more and more from the subconscious depths of the soul. We can see in what a gentle, tender form, imbued with the noblest qualities of the human soul, the Sibylline power of the Maid of Orléans is revealed."[114]

In the lecture referenced above, Steiner reflects upon a letter written during that period by an associate of Joan's named Percival Lord of

---

[113] Steiner, Rudolf. Christ and the Spiritual World: The Search for the Holy Grail, Lecture 5. January 1, 1914. Thus, we see this effect occur in Joan of Arc.

[114] Steiner, Rudolf. Christ and the Spiritual World: The Search for the Holy Grail. Lecture 6. January 2, 1914. This is abridged quote. There were six lectures delivered during this cycle. Thus, in this excerpt Steiner refers to "these lectures". The Atlantean reference here considers an ancient and inherited form of clairvoyance that was transformed in humanity over time and had faded away. This inherent form of clairvoyance was in the process of transforming, and falling away, by the time of the Christ event in 33AD.

Bonlamiulk to highlight the nature of her character, which draws a correlation to the qualities of a genuine Sybil.

> "This and much more has the Maid brought about, and with God's help she will accomplish still greater things. The girl is of appealing beauty and manly bearing; she speaks little and shows remarkable sagacity; when she speaks, she has a pleasing, delicately feminine voice. She eats little and abstains from wine. She takes pleasure in fine horses and weapons and admires well-accoutred and noble men.

> "To be obliged to meet and converse with large numbers of people is abhorrent to her; her tears often overflow; she loves a happy face, endures unheard of toil, and is so assiduous in the manipulation and bearing of weapons that she remains uninterruptedly for six days — day and night — in full armor. She says that the English have no right to France, and therefore — as she says — God has sent her to drive them out and conquer them, but only after previous warning. For the King she shows the deepest veneration; she says he is beloved by God, is under special protection, and will therefore be preserved. Of the Duke of Orléans, your nephew, she says that he will be delivered in a miraculous way, but only after a demand for his release has been made to the English who hold him prisoner."[115]

This is a peculiar description. From this, we can discern that Sibyls, or those who carry a Sybil-like quality, avoid alcohol, are abstemious, motivated, prudent and honorable, healthy, brave, shy, virtuous, well-mannered, compassionate, and are prepared to protect and defend their virtue. Staying in full armor for "six days – day and night" reveals Joan's dedication to the mission and her virtue. Furthermore, the letter refers to emotions. Joan was seen weeping openly for the French and English alike. She openly expresses joy in a happy face and is highly communicative. This duty to honor is revealed in the fact that Joan repeatedly was compelled to offer her enemies an option to surrender and leave before giving battle. At Orléans, for example, Joan wrote three letters (the first was on March 22,

---

[115] Ibid. This letter was written by a certain French noble loyal to Charles VII named "Percival, Lord of Bonlamiulk, Counselor and Chamberlain of the King of the French and of the Duke of Orléans, Seneschal of Berry." The letter was written at Biteromis on June 21, 1429 and was addressed to the Duke of Milan. Accounts at the retrial of 1456 later reveal that Joan slept in armor and experienced severe bruising as a result.

1429) to Lord Talbot. The final letter, dictated directly by Joan and addressed to Talbot stated:

> "You, men of England, who have no right in the kingdom of France, the King of Heaven sends word to you, and commands by me, Joan the Maid, that you leave your fortresses and return to your own country. Otherwise, I will produce a clash of arms to be eternally remembered. This is the third and last time I will write to you, and I will not write to you anymore. [116]
> Jesus Maria
> Joan the Maid"

This knightly form of conduct, which also carries with it a certain authority and confidence, goes against sound military thinking especially in the modern world. The essence of surprise, if it can be achieved, is a critical aspect of victory as history teaches us during times of war. However, Joan was not a dogmatic political or military leader. She was influenced and led by divine higher beings. Joan was, as the author contends, one who manifested the qualities of a Grail Knight within her. In the spirit of the legends of King Arthur, knightly conduct is a foundational aspect of becoming a genuine Knight in the Grail tradition. This means observing strict virtues and fighting honorably, bravely, and with compassion.

Joan, as revealed by Steiner, was a genuine bearer of the Christ impulse in the very core of her being. To be imbued with the Christ impulse in this fashion, she had to transform her lower impulses to the highest degree possible. This purification was something that she had earned, and carried forward, within her soul before being born. As a result, Joan would never have engaged the enemy in a dishonorable way. Her spiritual principles, which were permeated by the Christ, demanded that she find a path without bloodshed and that the enemy have every opportunity to withdraw without loss of life. Only a true sense of honor, and a sound spiritual conscience, compels one to undertake such an approach that surely came at the objections of many of her fellow French captains.

So, in Joan, we observe an individual who brought with her an inherited form of clairvoyance before being born that was cultivated through her karmic history and unique disposition. We observe one who was connected to nature and the elements in a spiritual way. We observe an individual

---

[116] Final letter shot by Joan by arrow into Fort Les Tourelles on May 5, 1429.

who proved her clairvoyant capabilities repeatedly by predicting the future accurately as was testified by many witnesses. We observe someone who was very much aware of her destiny to lead a world-historic mission while acting as a conduit for the Christ, Michael, and the Spiritual Hierarchies. This is revealed in her statement that she allegedly gave as she was leaving Vaucouleurs for Chinon when she was asked by a woman:

> "When she spoke of leaving, she was asked how she thought she could effect such a journey and escape the enemy. "I fear them not," she answered, "I have a sure road: if the enemy are on my road, I have God with me, Who knows how to prepare the way to the Lord Dauphin. I was born to do this."[117]

Contrary to some modern portrayals of Joan, there is no uncertainty in Joan's disposition whatsoever. She was aware of her mission and was fully committed to it. In Joan, we observe an individual of high character, courage, determination, and genuine spiritual vision. She came into the world to serve a higher purpose for humanity. As remarkable as it seems, Joan changed the map of Europe by way of the Christ forces within her.

> "...the Christ impulse worked itself into the soul of the simple country girl, The Maid of Orléans. It was she who caused the victory of the French over the English. Again, not the human mind nor the talents of military leaders were decisive factors in changing the map of Europe so magnificently, but rather the Christ impulse working itself into the subconscious of the Maid of Orléans and inspiring her to radiate its presence in all of history."[118]

> "Take the figure of the Maid of Orléans. In European history, the simple shepherd girl appears. She appeared in a remarkable way; there lived in her soul not only those forces, which are otherwise to be found in human beings, but the Christ Impulse works in this personality, enlivening and sustaining her through its mighty influence. She became a kind of representative of the Christ Impulse

---

[117] The English translation of the trial files from 1902. From the book: Jeanne d'Arc Maid of Orléans Deliverer of France. Edited by T. Douglas Murray, Deposition of Henri Leroyer Cartwright, formerly of Vaucouleurs.

[118] Steiner, Rudolf. The Great Virtues. The Golden Blade, Zürich, January 31, 1915. GA159.

itself for her time. This she was only able to do, because the Christ Impulse could enter and live within her."[119]

So, in light of these facts, both spiritual and historical, it is clear that Joan was something unique and served a special mission on behalf of the Christ, Michael, and the exalted beings of the spiritual worlds who oversee the destiny of humanity. To gain further insights into how this true Christian knight behaved, let us turn our attention to Joan's activities in the field which began in late 1428.

[119] Steiner, Rudolf. The Mystery of Death, Zurich, January 31, 1915.

Left: "Jeanne d'Arc" by Henri Chapu, circa 1870. Based on images revealed through the author's intuition, this sculpture of Jeanne is the closest resemblance to her actual appearance known. Modern portrayals of a frail child are fanciful and imaginative. Joan possessed an athletic form, was kind, brave, proactive, and generous. She was mature for her age and projected a certain perceptive glare through her eyes that seemed to pierce the veil of one's being but it was not hostile. The vast majority of historical prints, busts, and artistic images bear very little, if any, physical resemblance to Joan from a historical perspective.

Historical information has survived that provides insights into Joan's character as revealed through her trial, certain letters, official documents, and the testimony of those who testified at her retrial in 1456.[120] Surviving quotes and testimony of some of Joan's acquaintances, relatives, and friends who shared first-hand experiences with her reveal aspects of her character that are consistent, objective, and complimentary. The testimony and statements provided by her friends, acquaintances, captains, and nobles who knew her are consistent. They portray Joan in the same consistent manner. As testified by those who knew her, Joan is remembered as a devout, virtuous, pious, honest, friendly, brave, intuitive, assertive, active, and fair-minded young woman who was devoted to the church and the principle of French liberty.

---

[120] Joan's mother pressed for this investigation and she lived to see her daughter's name cleared at the conclusion of the retrial.

"Many times, I heard Messire Guillaume Fronte, in his lifetime Curé of Domrémy, say that Jeanne the Maid was a simple and good girl, pious, well-brought-up, and God-fearing, and without her like in the whole village. Often did she confess her sins; and, if she had had money, she would have given it to him, he told me, to say Masses."[121]

From a historical perspective, not much is known of Joan's childhood as she led a private life in a remote area. Information that has been passed down primarily through the transcript of the retrial of 1456, Jeanne was born in Domrémy in the Lorraine region of France known as the Duchy of Bar then under the domain of the Duc (Duke) de Lorraine to a peasant-farmer who held a minor official position on January 6, 1412. One of Joan's godfathers was the mayor of Domrémy. Joan appears to have been the fourth child of Jacques d'Arc (b. 1380-d. 1431 or 1440 as dates vary) and his wife Isabelle Romée (b. 1384-d. 1458). Joan had three older brothers named Jacquemin, Jean, and Pierre. She may have had one sister, perhaps younger, named Catherine. Joan had at least four sets of godparents from her home village. Her father's burial location is lost to history and according to records, her mother is interred at the Cathédrale Notre-Dame de Paris.

The village of Domrémy la-Pucelle, renamed in Joan's honor after her death, existed at the crossroads of disputed territory between four feudal French Dukes. As the war carried on, the town became a disputed area between the French, English, and Burgundians. It seems that Joan's father managed to secure agreements with the French feudal lords in whose jurisdiction the village existed for protection that appears to have provided some measure of protection. But, as testified at the Trial of Rehabilitation in 1455, the village was burned down at least once.

"Up to her departure, she was properly brought up; she was a chaste maiden, and of modest habits. She frequented with great devotion, churches and holy places; and, after the village of Domrémy was burned, she went on Feast Days to attend Mass at Greux."[122]

---

[121] The Trial of Rehabilitation, The English translation of the trial files from 1902. From the book: Jeanne d'Arc Maid of Orléans Deliverer of France. Edited by T. Douglas Murray, the Deposition of Messire Etienne of Sionne, Curé of the Parish Church of Roncessey-sous-Neufchâteau.

[122] Ibid. From the deposition of Beatrix Widow of Estellin, laborer, of Domrémy 1455.

However, raiding parties were regularly seen throughout the area and the War for France became a part of Joan's life. One story persists that her family was driven from her home on at least one occasion. Joan was well-known for her chastity, preferred to sing and pray instead of dancing, and spent many hours in work, prayer, and took regular confession at the local church in her village.

> "She never swore, and, to affirm strongly, contented herself with saying, "Without fail!" She was no dancer; and, sometimes, when the others were singing and dancing, she went to prayer. Jeannette was fond of work, spinning, looking after the house, and, when necessary, taking her turn at minding her father's cattle."[123]

Joan respected the church and was devout in her faith. She was loyal to her parents, refused to marry, or her father prevented it, which no doubt rubbed many of the paternal and traditional men the wrong way during that time period when women were viewed as commodities and were typically married off at a young age. Her father, by all accounts, kept Joan close to him and watched over her diligently almost to the point of oppression. Joan prayed daily, longed for the church bells that rang in the nearby church (reputedly sometimes dropping to her knees when they were heard),[124] was a dedicated garment weaver who was proud of her ability[125] and was rarely, if ever, seen loitering about town. Rumors and legends regarding the so-called Fairy Tree, or Ladies' Tree, appear to be exaggerated and taken out of context although one account states that Joan accompanied her friends to that social spot when she was a child. Contrary to legend, Joan never admitted to seeing fairies by the natural spring near her home.

> "She had heard several old folk say, not of her family, that the fairies frequented it (the tree); and she had heard her godmother Jeanne, wife (of the mayor of the village of Domrémy), say that she had seen them there. Whether this was true, she does not know. She said that

---

[123] Ibid. Deposition of Jeannette Widow of Thiesselin of Viteaux, formerly clerk at Neufchâteau.

[124] Dominique Jacob, a priest of a nearby parish, testified at her retrial that "...sometimes when they rang the bells for Compline in the village church, she would go down on her knees; and it seemed to me that she said her prayers with devotion."

[125] "Asked if in her youth she had learned any craft, she said yes, to sew and spin: and in sewing and spinning, she feared no woman in Rouen." Barrett, W.P. The Trial of Joan of Arc ,1932.

she herself had never seen a fairy, as far as she knew, either at the tree or anywhere else."[126]

"This tree, since ancient times, has been called the Ladies' Tree, and it used to be said that the ladies who are called fairies went there. However, I never heard it said that anyone had ever seen one. The boys and girls of the town are accustomed to go to this tree and to the Rains Spring on the Sunday of Laetare Jerusalem called (Sunday) of the Springs, and they take bread with them. I went with Joan the Maid, for she was my comrade, and other girls and young men to the Fairies' Tree on Springs Sunday. There we ate, we danced, we played; I have seen nuts (walnuts) taken to the tree and to the Springs."[127]

Joan's appreciation of the ringing of the church bells was something that she enjoyed and looked forward to each day. During the Trial of Rehabilitation, it was revealed that Joan once tracked down Perrin Drappier, the churchwarden at Domrémy, lectured and then offered him a trade of "flat cakes" when she felt that he was not performing his duties well enough;

"When I forgot to ring for Service, Jeanne scolded me, saying I had done wrong; and she promised to give me some of the wool of her flock ("flat cakes") if I would ring more diligently..."[128]

Joan's reputation as a noble-hearted and simple woman of faith was recounted repeatedly by the testimony of those who knew her best, many of whom served with her on the campaign against the English. Joan was seen helping the poor, rarely playing, obsessively going to church for prayer and confession, and otherwise minding her chores:

"She was very hospitable to the poor, and would even sleep on the hearth in order that the poor might lie in her bed. She was not fond

---

[126] Abridged quote from The Trial of Joan of Arc being the verbatim report of the proceedings from the Orléans manuscript, 1956.

[127] Excerpt from the transcript of the retrial in 1456 by one of Joan's acquaintances.

[128] The Retrial of Joan of Arc. The English translation of the trial files from 1902. From the book: Jeanne d'Arc Maid of Orléans Deliverer of France. Edited by T. Douglas Murray Deposition of Perrin Le Drapier of Domrémy, Churchwarden of the Parish Church and Bell-ringer.

of playing, at which we, her companions, complained. She liked work; and would spin, labour with her father, look after the house, and sometimes mind the sheep. She was never seen idling in the roads; she was more often in Church at prayer."[129]

The testimony provided during Joan's retrial is consistent and provides insights into the character of one who, as was revealed by Dr. Steiner, was permeated by the Christ. Whatever peculiarities emerge are, in some way, a manifestation of her virtues and not vices. From the testimony that has survived, not a single comment survived that cast Joan in a negative light. Her friends, in fact, accused her of being too pious:

"My father's house joined the house of Jacques d'Arc: so I knew her well. We often spun together, and together worked at the ordinary house-duties, whether by day or night. She was a good Christian, of good manners and well brought up. She loved the Church, and went there often, and gave alms from the goods of her father. She was a good girl, simple and pious—so much so that I and her companions told her she was too pious."[130]

In another instance, we see an example of Joan's reputation of her absolute intolerance of profanity. After chastising the men of the army regularly, they eventually acquiesced out of fear of Joan's reprimands.

"Many times, when the Duke d'Alençon swore or blasphemed before her, I heard her reprove him. As a rule, no one in the army dared swear or blaspheme before her, for fear of being reprimanded."[131]

And, as is well known amongst those who are familiar with Joan's life, we see yet another example of Joan's virtue when she disallowed women to follow the army in any form. She did not punish them, rather she simply advised them to go home. Based on all of the evidence that I have reviewed, Joan never physically harmed anyone. Traditionally, the armies in the ancient and medieval world had camp followers and this trailing group of people often included wives, families, various kinds of tradesmen, and prostitutes.

[129]Ibid. Deposition of Isabellette Wife of Gerardin, laborer, of Epinal.
[130]Ibid. Deposition of Mengette Wife of Jean Joya.
[131]Ibid. Deposition of Louis de Contes. Page to Joan of Arc.

"She would have no women in her army. One day, near Château-Thierry, seeing the mistress of one of her followers riding on horseback, she pursued her with her sword, without striking her at all; but with gentleness and charity she told her she must no longer be found amongst the soldiers, otherwise she would suffer for it."[132]

So, Joan also played the role of a mother figure to those that she met on the campaign...if she felt it was necessary. This is in perfect alignment with what one would expect from someone her high, and yet gentle, motherly nature. Accounts such as these are repeated throughout the Trial of Rehabilitation in 1456 shall not be repeated in totality as the text of the trial is available for reading elsewhere. With regards to Joan's visions, she revealed a good deal of information regarding how she experienced them. In her testimony at the Trial of 1431 in Rouen, Joan claims that her spiritual visions began when she was 13 years old in her father's garden. Most likely this would have occurred during the years of 1424-1425AD as she was approximately 19 years old at the time of her death in 1431AD.

"And she said that, from the age of thirteen, she received revelation from Our Lord by a voice which taught her how to behave. And the first time she was greatly afraid. And she said that the voice came that time at noon, on a summer's day, a fast day, when she was in her father's garden, and that the voice came on her right side, in the direction of the church. And she said that the voice was hardly ever without a light, which was always in the direction of the voice.

"She said further that, after she had heard it three times, she knew that it was the voice of an angel. She said also that this voice had always taken good care of her...that it taught her how to behave. And it said to her that she ought to go often to church. And later it said to her that it was necessary that she should go into France. And it said to her two or three times a week that she must leave and go into France. And that her father knew nothing of her going. And with this, it said to her that she must hurry and go and raise the siege of Orléans; and that she should go to Robert de Baudricourt, captain of Vaucouleurs; and that he would give her men to accompany her.

[132]Ibid.

"To which she answered that she was only a poor woman, who knew nothing of riding or of making war. And after these words, she went to an uncle's house, where she stayed a week, after which her uncle brought her to Robert de Baudricourt..."[133]

Thus, up to the time when Joan departed her home village for the bastion at Vaucouleurs in 1428 to obtain permission to go to Chinon to visit Charges VII, Joan led a pretty stable and basic life as a loyal, good-natured, and high-minded farmgirl. What is not known, nor can be known from any surface level review, are the inner aspects that surrounded Joan's birth, the context of her destiny that led her to that point in time, and the true nature of the voices that had come to her and insisted that she travel to Chinon on a broader mission and why that task was necessary for her, and her alone, to undertake. After all, the angelic beings who came to Joan could have gone to any number of soldiers, knights, captains, or political leaders...or could they...

For the answers, let us turn to the insights brought to us by Dr. Rudolf Steiner where we find that Joan, and Joan alone, was the bearer of a special spiritual impulse and that she was selected, as so, a broader task for the world, to fulfill a broader spiritual mission. Thus, no one else could have carried out her mission at that specific point in time...

---

[133] The Retrial of 1456. The English translation of the trial files from 1902. From the book: Jeanne d'Arc Maid of Orléans Deliverer of France. Edited by T. Douglas Murray.

"Joan of Arc" circa 1879 by Jules Bastien-Lepage.

Joan's Birth, Youth, and Mission in Light of Spiritual Science

Joan was an individual who incarnated at a specific moment in time for a specific purpose.[134] The nature of her birth and childhood, as a rural farm woman in a small French village, was simply the path by which she came into the world to fulfill a broader mission. It is, perhaps, an interesting destiny that one of the pivotal spiritual leaders of that time incarnated in a rural French backwater as an illiterate farm girl. That is one of the true mysteries of Joan's life. However, throughout history, many people have been born in remote places that few people have ever heard of, and later emerged to influence world events.[135] Thus, any egotism or perception of

---

[134] All people incarnate with a specific mission and purpose at any given moment in time based on their destinies and karma, but Joan's purpose was of a broader, global importance.
[135] General Dwight D. Eisenhower, for example, was born in the small rural town of Denison, Texas. General Douglas Macarthur was born in Little Rock, Arkansas, Admiral Chester Nimitz was born in Fredericksburg, Texas, and so on.

the superiority, in terms of geography, of one's place of birth is meaningless.

With regards to the nature of Joan's birth, Dr. Steiner reveals that a unique spiritual event occurred that is unknown to the masses. The fact that Joan was born on the Epiphany, or January 6, reflects a connection to the birth of Christ Jesus, but the hidden and true spiritual nature of that specific date as it pertains to Joan of Arc contains a much more profound significance.

As perceived in the Akashic Records or Cosmic Script, Steiner reveals that in the period of time before Joan's birth, a special event over occurred over the 13-day period between Christmas and the Epiphany on January 6. Over the course of two weeks, during the final stages of Joan's birth cycle, the Christ imbued in Joan's soul subtle and powerful forces while she effectively slept in her mother's womb. Dr. Steiner refers to this event as a "natural initiation".

> "We would have to notice if anything similar could have taken place as a natural initiation with the Maid of Orléans if the soul of the Maid of Orléans had been inspired in the nights from the 25th December to the 6th January. In the course of life, it seems that such a matter cannot be verified that the Maid of Orléans also was once during twelve or thirteen days from the 25th December to the 6th January in a sleep-like state in which the Christ Impulse would have worked on her, so that she would be able to work as a human being only like the cover of the Christ Impulse on the battlefields of France. Nevertheless, it was that way. For there is a time which — if the karma of the concerning individuality makes it possible — can be filled with such a sleep-like state."[136]

Over the course of 13 days, Joan received a transformational spiritual impulse directly from the Christ in her soul that can only occur once during the calendar year on January 6.[137] Thus, while Joan was not made aware of her mission until she reached the age of maturity by way of her spiritual guardians, she had been prepared for it before her birth through Christ, Michael, and karma.

---

[136] Steiner, Rudolf, The Mystery of Death, The Threefold Being, Linz, May 18, 1915.
[137] Steiner, Rudolf. Brunetto Latini Lecture, January 30th, 1915. GA 161.

"The soul of the Maid of Orléans had to be kindled for a great historic mission. There had to be present in her soul the impulses that surge and weave their way throughout the world with the Christ-Impulse. They had to be there in her soul. How should they enter her? They could indeed have entered her, if at some time in her life...if she had slept for the thirteen days after Christmas and had awakened on the 6th of January. And so indeed it was...in a certain sense she underwent in sleep this time which is so favorable to Initiation. She underwent it in the last thirteen days of her embryonal life. She was borne by her mother, so as to pass through the Christmas season in the body of her mother in the last thirteen days of her embryo life. For she was born on the 6th January. That is the birthday of Joan of Arc. Thus, she passed through the very time in which the spiritual forces weave and work most strongly in the Earth's aura." [138]

Thus, a unique window opens during the calendar year when a focused concentration of the astral forces of the earth intensifies in such a way that can enable an event such as described by Steiner if, and only if, a soul has the right disposition for it. This is due to regular cycles as the earth sleeps, and wakes, just as people do. The earth is most awake, in spiritual terms, during the period leading up to the Epiphany in the winter months. This window, which begins during the anniversary date of Christ's birth, occurs during the darkest time of the year when the days are at their shortest length. In spiritual terms, the Sun influences of the Christ are at their height as they permeate the darkness...

"Old legends tell us that over Christmas, up to January 6, people have had special experiences, because at this time the life of the earth, and the inner forces of the earth, are most concentrated. Those who have the right disposition for it, experience then in fact the spiritual forces within the earthly forces. Countless legends describe this. The best time for this covers thirteen days before January 6th."

In another lecture, Dr. Steiner states:

"During the day's twenty-four hours, this earth sleeps and is awake just as we are. We must familiarize ourselves with the fact that the state of wakefulness on earth occurs during the winter, and the state

[138] Ibid.

of sleep during the summer. The earth spirit is most awake in these twelve or thirteen days from Christmas to the Epiphany. In ancient ages when, as you know from the various presentations in my lecture series, human beings elevated themselves to a sort of dreamlike clairvoyance to reach a spiritual understanding of the world, in those ages the most favorable time for this process was summer.

"Thus, it is quite natural that whoever wants to elevate himself to spiritual heights by means of a more dreamlike clairvoyance will have an easier time of it during the summer, when the earth is asleep. Therefore, St. John's midsummer-day was in ancient ages the most propitious time to raise the soul to the spiritual level. The old way of spiritual interaction with the earth has been replaced by a more conscious elevation that can best be reached during the earth's wakefulness.

"For this reason, legends inform us that unusually endowed people, who are particularly suited by their karmas, pass into an extraordinary state of consciousness that resembles sleep, but only on the surface. its inner quality is such that it can be inspired by those forces that elevate human beings to the domain we call the spirit world. A beautiful Norwegian legend tells us that Olaf Åsteson, in church on Christmas Eve, falls into a sleeplike state and when he awakens on January 6 is able to relate the experiences he had in this condition. This Norwegian legend does in fact describe the experiences that one perceives first as the soul world — and then as something that feels like the spirit world, but with everything being expressed as images, as imaginative forms."[139]

There are many legends regarding Joan's youth. Steiner does not address each of them, but in one instance he relates the reality that while legends relate a tale of villagers being stirred up with the portent of on the night of her birth, the reality is different.

"It was during the night of the Epiphany of Our Lord (January 6, Twelfth Night), when men are wont most joyfully to recall the acts of Christ that she first saw the light in this mortal life. And, wonderful

---

[139] Steiner, Rudolf. Christ in Relation to Lucifer and Ahriman, Linz, May 18, 1915 GA 159.

> to relate, the poor inhabitants of the place were seized with an
> inconceivable joy. And though ignorant of the birth of the Maid, they
> rushed hither and thither in search of what might be the new event."
> [140]

> "Therefore, we need not wonder, if even outer documents relate
> that on that January 6, 1412, the villagers ran hither and thither,
> feeling that something momentous had happened, — though what
> it was that happened on that 6th of January they did not know until
> a later time, when the Maid of Orléans fulfilled her mission."[141]

As was the case with the revelation of Christ's life, not everyone who came into contact with the Christ recognized Him. Thus, most people were not aware of the true nature of Joan's mission, or the being of the Christ working through her. Most people began to perceive the importance and reality of her mission only after her death, although many of those who served with her recognized Joan as a leader of special significance. Many who came into contact with her were transformed and sensed something within her that touched them in a very personal way.

Joan received detailed information from her spiritual guardians through an inherited form of clairvoyance or psychic ability, that was perhaps intensified through her natural initiation before being born. Through that faculty, which others obviously cannot share in a communal way, spiritual beings provided her with guidance, instructions of healthy living, and eventually a greater mission to fulfill. Unbeknownst to the unassuming, polite, nice young girl who spent her time in prayer and chores, Joan was advised to take on a mission by her spiritual guides, whom she stated later in the Trial of 1431 were St. Michael, St. Gabriel, St. Margaret, and St. Catherine. She also claimed to have visions of the Holy Mother and other angelic beings. These messengers, and leaders, were her constant companions since the age of 13. She stated that they pressed her to pursue a special task for France.

> "...In the time of Joan of Arc, it was necessary for the impulse out of
> which she was to act (the Christ Impulse) to be born out of the
> gentlest, the most subtle powers of the human soul. Just consider:

---

[140] This story emerged from a letter written by Percival Lord of Bonlamiulk also known as Perceval de Boulainvilliers.
[141] Ibid.

she was a shepherd girl living a very simple, natural life, with nature at her most idyllic. She was very young when her visions came to her, and through the Imaginations given to her she had a direct link with the spiritual world. Out of her inner being she was to bring forth everything that was to be the foundation from which she acted, she was to let it grow forth from her inner being. And not only this, but it was necessary for very special circumstances to be brought about so that through the most subtle powers inherent in the human soul her mission could be imprinted in her soul, in her very heart of hearts."[142]

During her life, the testimony provided by those who knew her at the Trial of Rehabilitation in 1456 clarifies that many who knew her in her youth surely did not recognize her as someone carrying a special impulse, or mission, within her. Later, many of Joan's acquaintances, friends, the captains, soldiers, and villagers alike perceived something unique in Joan, which manifested as predictions and confidence, although they could not say what. Some looked in her eyes and recognized her as a saint. Joan was perceived by many of the French soldiers as a chosen delegate from God and many of them came to accept that she, and they who followed her, were on a divine mission. Joan's peculiar nature stood out, but her prognostications and predictions that so repeatedly came true astonished and convinced many who came into contact with her. Some followed her to the bitter end on faith alone sensing that she was the bearer of a certain special mission, the precise nature of which they did not understand. Many of the French nobles, commoners, and rank and file genuinely looked upon Joan as a special talisman and prophetess sent by God guiding the army forwards to victory. Regardless of one's disposition, either for or against, many were transformed by her in many hidden ways.[143]

---

[142] Steiner, Rudolf, The Destinies of Individuals and of Nations, Lecture 5, The Nature of the Christ Impulse and the Michaelic Sprit Serving It – 2.

[143] We must remember that there are always those who are sensitive to the Christ impulse who react receptively or antagonistically. Thus, Joan, was surrounded by friends who were inspired by her as well as her enemies in the French, English, and Burgundian sides where violently antagonized by her.

"All the soldiers held her as sacred. So well did she bear herself in warfare, in words and in deeds, as a follower of God, that no evil could be said of her."[144]

Joan states during her trial that her spiritual communications began at the age of 13 in her father's garden. However, this does not mean that she did not have clairvoyant experiences during her youth that, perhaps, she chose not to reveal. We must remember that a moderately intelligent person would never reveal the inner substance of all of their life experiences to a hostile court of antagonists and accusers as they stood trial for sorcery during the age of the inquisition.

Joan was a mature and discerning individual who was well aware of the conflicted loyalties of the peoples of France, including those in her village, who bore disparate sympathies to the Burgundians, English, and the French. Surely Joan learned early to keep her spiritual communications a closely guarded secret, the substance of which she revealed only when the moment was appropriate. Because of her virtue, Joan was compelled by honesty and a duty to the truth. However, she also possessed a covenant with her spiritual guides who advised her on what, and what not, to reveal to others. As a result, Joan revealed the substance of only some of her spiritual communications during the Trial of 1431. For example:

"When I was thirteen years old, I had a voice from God to help me govern my conduct. And the first time I was very fearful. And came this voice, about the hour of noon, in the summer-time, in my father's garden; I had not fasted on the eve preceding that day. I heard the voice on the right-hand side, towards the church; and rarely do I hear it without a brightness. This brightness comes from the same side as the voice is heard. It is usually a great light. When I came to France, often I heard this voice. The voice was sent to me by God and, after I had thrice heard this voice, I knew that it was the voice of an angel. This voice has always guarded me well and I have always understood it clearly."[145]

---

[144] The Retrial of 1456. The English translation of the trial files from 1902. From the book: Jeanne d'Arc Maid of Orléans Deliverer of France. Edited by T. Douglas Murray, Deposition of Maître Jean Barbin Doctor of Laws, King's Advocate.

[145] Excerpt from the transcript of the Trial of Joan of Arc.

Steiner clarifies and confirms that Joan perceived her spiritual communications clearly and that they were, in fact, objectively valid. He stated that Joan's visions were necessarily clothed in the imagery of the times, through Joan's cultural perspective, yet he also states that they were genuine and that Joan perceived them clearly.

> "This young girl, certainly not highly educated even by the standards of her time, suddenly, before she is twenty years old, feels in the autumn of 1428 that spiritual Powers of the super-sensible worlds are speaking to her. True, she clothes these Powers in forms that are familiar to her, so that she is seeing them through the medium of her own mental images; but that does not do away with the reality of these Powers. Picture to yourselves that she knows that super-sensible Powers are guiding her will towards a definite point."[146]

In recent times, with the advent of modern psychiatry and psychology, which is still in its infancy in true spiritual terms, articles and studies regarding alleged mental illness, epilepsy, or other psychoses are based on a form of bias and egotism to discredit Joan and genuine spiritual experience.[147] After all, even in today's modern world with advanced technologies at our disposal, no one can prove or disprove the substance of a genuine spiritual vision, thus each person addressees the topic based on one's background, experience, and egotism.

Thus, while the vast majority of us today do not possess the faculty to perceive, and see, the true nature of Joan's mission that cannot be proven based on modern forms of forensic analysis, she nonetheless, as confirmed through the perception of a genuine spiritual initiate in Rudolf Steiner and the proof substantiated by the truthfulness of the predictions that she repeatedly revealed during her life by those who knew her, that Joan was imbued with certain spiritual powers that others lacked. Steiner confirms

---

[146] Steiner, Rudolf. Occult History, Lecture 2, Stuttgart, December 28, 1910

[147] In the case of Joan, these studies and efforts are driven by Ahrimanic influences who seek to steer humanity away from genuine spiritual ideas, principles, and historical facts. In the modern age, the field of medicine, with all of its innovations, has also become corrupted by wealth seekers at the institutional level, as permeated by the pharmaceutical industry. In the ongoing malaise of varying conflicts of interest in the pharmaceutical industry and the sphere of modern psychiatry, which are often rooted in egotism and self-interest, there is hardly anything that cannot, in some way, be considered a form of mental illness in modern academic and clinical terms.

that it was the forces of the Christ and the Archangel Michael that led her to the completion of her mission.

> "An event which reveals the inpouring of the Spiritual into the earthly events in a most clear and radiant way is the appearance and subsequent history of Joan of Arc, the Maid of Orléans. impulses for what she does lie in the deep, subconscious foundations of her soul. She follows dim inspirations from the spiritual world. On the Earth there is confusion and disorder, through which the age of the Spiritual (Consciousness) Soul is to be hindered. Michael has to prepare from the spiritual world his later mission; this he is able to do where his impulses are received into human souls. Such a soul lives in the Maid of Orléans. And Michael also worked through many other souls, although this was possible only in a minor degree and is less apparent in outer historical life. In events such as the war between England and France he met with opposition from his Ahrimanic adversary... In our last lecture we spoke of the Luciferic adversary (which) Michael found at the same time. And indeed, this adversary is particularly apparent in the course of events following upon the appearance of the Maid of Orléans..."[148]

It is important for a researcher to consider that in order to approach the mystery of Joan's life and mission, we must try to grasp the mystical, or cosmic, nature of the Christ who works through many mysterious pathways including the Archangel Michael. He does not need to rely on the erudition of the educated to fulfill His task. Clearly, an advanced education was not required at that point in time to fulfill his task. During Joan's life, theologians had begun the movement of contemplating the nuances of theological argument, the substance of which Joan did not need to know, understand, or was necessary for her mission. Thus, these theological debates of the day that consumed men's minds were not important.

> "One might say that while the learned people disputed over many things — for example, they already began to dispute on the question as to whether the Holy Supper should be eaten in this or in that form, and whether this or that should be interpreted by this or that formula, — while the learned people showed that their

---

[148] Steiner, Rudolf. <u>Anthroposophical Leading Thoughts</u>. The Life, Nature, and Cultivation of Anthroposophy, The Michael Mystery, Letters to Members, Second Study: How the Michael Forces Work in the Earliest Unfolding of the Spiritual Soul. GA26, 1924AD.

understanding, their conscious understanding could not (comprehend or approach) the Christ-Impulse, this impulse worked through the medium of a simple country maid, through the Maid of Orléans; it worked in such a way as to mold and shape the history of Europe. The influence of the Christ-Impulse does not depend on the comprehension we have for it. I might say that the Christ-Impulse penetrated into the Maid of Orléans through Michael, its representative."[149]

Based on the historical background and insights regarding Joan's mission and task, it is clear that her birth and youth bore special significance for fulfilling a unique and important mission. Every peculiar nuance of Joan's youth is not known, nor is it important for a researcher to know those things. In light of historical facts and Dr. Steiner's spiritual insights, it is important for us to know that Joan was an integrated part of a critical, unique, and special event that occurred and directly connected to the Christ, the Archangel Michael, and the Spiritual Hierarchies who were working on behalf of humanity.

---

[149] Steiner, Rudolf. Spiritual Science, a Necessity for the Present Time. Nuremberg, March 13, 1915. Parenthesis are mine. Some text appears to missing from the transcription of this lecture.

Chapter 6: Joan in the Field

"We journeyed eleven days, always riding towards the said town of Chinon. On the way, I asked her many times if she would really do all she said. "Have no fear," she answered us, "what I am commanded to do, I will do; my brothers in Paradise have told me how to act: it is four or five years since my brothers in Paradise and my Lord—that is, God—told me that I must go and fight in order to regain the kingdom of France."[150]

It is not the intent of this study to review all of the historical aspects of Joan's mission during the years 1429-1431AD. This chapter provides an overview of certain important aspects of events with the intent of demonstrating continuity between historical events and Joan's spiritual mission. Many examples of Joan's prognostications exist as were documented by eyewitness testimonies in the transcript of the retrial of 1452-56 and some of these will be referenced here as they reveal Joan's commitment to her virtue, mission, and spiritual faculties.[151] As one reviews this period of Joan's life, one cannot escape the sense of the light of hope and destiny that generated tremendous and miraculous victories as brought forth by a genuine hero that is immediately followed by a sense of a tremendous and unnecessary defeat and tragedy that finds its low point, as it were, in Joan's betrayal and painful martyrdom.[152]

The major events of the years 1429-1431 can be viewed at a high level in the following outline.[153] What is painfully obvious from this timeline, and ultimately tragic, is that Joan led Charles VII and the French peoples from one victory to the next and a flawless sweep began that was driving the English out of France by force in very quick time. The war had dragged on for 82 years prior to 1428 and France had reached a low point and was on the verge of annihilation. The Hundred Year's War which, in French terms, was nothing more than a series of failures and minor victories spread out

---

[150] The English translation of the trial files from 1902. From the book: <u>Jeanne d'Arc Maid of Orléans Deliverer of France.</u> Edited by T. Douglas Murray. Deposition of Jean de Novelemport Knight, Jean de Metz.

[151] A detailed timeline of the Hundred Years' War and the activities of Joan during her public mission is documented in Appendix A.

[152] The great mystery of Christ's victory follows a similar path and is shared by those who manifest it.

[153] Refer to Appendix A for a detailed timeline of the Hundred Years' War.

over several decades. During the retrial of 1456, some testified that all of the French captains agreed that the City of Orléans, for example, could not have been taken without the assistance of divine powers.

- Journey to Vaucouleurs.
- Meeting with Charles VII at Chinon,
- Examination and questioning at Poitiers.
- Journey to Tours to recover the Sword of Catherine.
- Victory at the City of Orléans.

"The Loire Valley Campaign"

- Victory at the Town of Jargeau.
- Securing of the fortified bridge at Meung-Sur-Loire was a critical tactical bridge.
- Victory at the Town of Beaugency.
- Victory at the Battle of Patay. Considered by some historians as the apex victory of the campaign.
- Victory at the Town of Troyes.
- Victory at the Town of Chalons-sur-Marne.
- Joan escorts Charles to Reims for his Coronation.
- Victory at the Town of Soissons.
- Victory at the Town of Château-Thierry.
- Attack of Paris and withdrawal, per the orders of Charles VII. Joan is wounded and removed from the battle against her orders. On the orders of Charles, the army is then disbanded.
- Joan is elevated to nobility. She spends the winter at the Royal court at Sully where she is kept under observation by Charles's closest advisors.
- Siege of La Charité-sur-Loire fails.
- Victory at the Town of Melun.
- Joan is captured at the Battle of Compiègne where she attempts to lift the siege of the Burgundians. The draw bridge is raised just in the nick of time before she can get inside as she protects the rear-guard of a small French force that is on the retreat back to the city.
- Joan is sold to the English by the Burgundians and moved to Rouen.
- The Trial and Joan's Execution.

After a series of victories, and for unknown reasons at the time, Charles ordered a halt to Joan's miraculous progress at the end of the year 1429 and disbanded the army. Based on the author's experience, and a long and diligent study of history, it is the author's view that this kind of behavior is always the result of secret agreements and parlays with the enemy or those who conspire with the enemy during times of war. It is, without any need for forensic proof, a sure indication of timidity, corruption, and/or ulterior motives. History reveals that Charles was under the heavy influence of several corrupted advisors who, as Steiner confirms, were motivated by jealousy. One man, in particular, was aligned to Burgundian interests.[154]

This envy was the direct result of Joan's successes and influence over the king. It appears that either Charles had no confidence in himself or was given poor and/or false advice by his counselors and thus retreated into the safety of his vacillation. His father certainly suffered from some form of mental impairment based on history's perspective of the man, but how that disability carried forward into Charles, if it all, is unknown to history. It does appear that he was weak-willed, indecisive, and preferred not to fight. Whatever the case, the situation deteriorated to the point of incomprehension when Joan was *allowed* to be captured by the Burgundians. Joan, it appears, was operating without full royal support and was led into a trap. This was accomplished by not providing her with proper support and supplies, which Charles had done the prior year.

Based on historical records, Steiner's insights, and the author's limited intuition, it is the view of the author that Joan was a strong-willed and kindly personality, never shirked from her duty and was a genuine leader of men who led from the front, as it were, and never from the rear. Although some biographies portray Joan as more of a titular, or symbolic, leader of the French army, the reality is that Joan was frequently seen on the front lines with her soldiers leading them on during combat, guarding and monitoring their moral life as only a virtuous mother would, and placing herself in harm's way having been wounded on at least two occasions. She always preferred to be in the vanguard, or main body, of the army.[155]

---

[154] One of the men responsible for Joan's demise at that time were a certain Georges de la Trémoille (1382-1446) who as advisor to King Charles VII who later fell out of favor and was banished from court.

[155] An army in the ancient, middle age, and medieval context was typically divided into four aspects; left, right, center (vanguard), and a rear guard that typically included the baggage train and supplies.

It is, perhaps, Joan's reputation as a mother figure that has stuck to her biography in the minds of devoted Catholics and people who take heed of their virtues. Joan was a soldier, it is true, but she also was a devoted Catholic and an individual who took her virtues, and the virtues of others, very seriously. It is obvious from accounts provided during the retrial of 1452-1456 that Joan did not ignore the poor behavior of others and, in fact, reproved them for it. She set a very high standard by her virtues and thus gained the admiration of those who followed her.

> "She lived honorably, most soberly as to food and drink, was chaste and devout, hearing Mass daily, and confessing often, communicating with fervent devotion every week. She reproved the soldiers when they blasphemed or took God's Name in vain; also, when they did any evil or violence. I never observed in her aught deserving reproof, and from her manner of life and actions I believe she was inspired by God."[156]

> "I have seen Jeanne, at the Elevation of the Host, weeping many tears. I remember well that she induced the soldiers to confess their sins; and I indeed saw that, by her instigation and advice, La Hire and many of his company came to confession."[157]

And, while safe-guarding the virtues of others, Joan was seen reprimanding people on occasion who took the Lord's name in vain:

> "I remember well to have seen and heard, one day, a great lord, walking along the street (in Orléans), begin to swear and blaspheme God; which, when Jeanne saw and heard, she was much perturbed, and went up to the lord who was swearing, and, taking him by the neck, said, "Ah! master, do you deny Our Lord and Master? In God's Name, you shall unsay your words before I leave you." And then, as

---

[156] The English translation of the trial files from 1902. From the book: Jeanne d'Arc Maid of Orléans Deliverer of France. Edited by T. Douglas Murray, Deposition of Guillaume de Ricarville Seigneur, Steward to the King.

[157] Ibid. Deposition of Maître Pierre Compaing Priest, Licentiate in Law, Canon of Saint-Aignan. Captain Étienne de Vignolles, also known as "La Hire" (1390-1443), is remembered as being one of the roughest of Joan's captains who used profanity regularly. After spending time with Joan, who reprimanded him for his poor language and, after witnessing her devotions and spiritual faculties in action, La Hire was inspired to cease using profanities and attended mass regularly.

I saw, the said lord repented and amended his ways, at the exhortation of the said Maid."[158]

Joan's mission into the public sphere began during the summer of 1428 at the age of 16, when Joan had fully embraced the breadth and calling of her task, destiny, and spiritual mission as it was delivered by her spiritual guides through her clairvoyance faculties. She proceeded to the first waypoint, as it were, when she asked her uncle (some claim this man was a cousin or godfather) named Durand Lassois (or Luxart) to escort her to the nearby town of Vaucouleurs so that she could petition the local garrison commander, a would-be French knight of lower noble rank named Robert de Baudricourt, for an armed escort to take her to the French Royal Court at Chinon to formally petition the French King Charles VII to engage the English in battle who were besieging the fortified City of Orléans.

Baudricourt's humiliating response to her request to petition Charles VII in Chinon did not deter Joan. Baudricourt suggested that Joan should be sent home to her father to "box her ears" as a silly woman...or something to that effect.

> "When the Maid saw that Sir Robert did not want to send her to the place where the Dauphin was, she herself handed me my cloak and told me that she wished to depart. And withdrawing, I took her to Saint Nicholas, and when she was there she went with a safe-conduct to the lord Charles, Duke of Lorraine, and when the lord Charles saw her, he spoke with her and gave her four francs, which she showed me. Then Joan went back to Vaucouleurs, and the people of the town bought her men's clothing, breeches, gaiters, and all that she needed; and Jacques Alain of Vaucouleurs and I bought her a horse for the price of twelve francs, out of our own pockets. However, my lord Robert de Baudricourt had the money paid back to us afterward. And after that jean de Metz, Bertrand de Poulengy, Colet de Vienne, and Richard L' Archer (the archer), with two servants of Jean de Metz and Bertrand, took Joan to the place where the Dauphin was."[159]

---

[158] The Retrial off 1456. The English translation of the trial files from 1902. From the book: Jeanne d'Arc Maid of Orléans Deliverer of France. Edited by T. Douglas Murray, Deposition of Reginalde, widow of Jean Huré.
159

After that incident, Joan stayed with a nearby relative while her uncle returned to Domrémy. Evidently, on the third try, which occurred in January of 1429, Joan managed to sway Robert to support her. There are various accounts of how she accomplished this, including sending messages to villages to rally behind her as the fulfillment of the Maid of Lorraine prophecy that opened his eyes, as it were, but accounts vary. Whatever the case, history reveals that Joan somehow convinced Robert and, given Joan's spiritual abilities, it seems probable that she used her powers of clairvoyance to convince him that she was a genuine messenger from God. The skirmish at the Battle of the Herrings[160] was yet another defeat for the French and some have speculated that the defeat motivated Robert, but even that turn of events would not be enough to convince a man of his rank to send a simple farm woman to the king on an official warrant without definitive proof. So, something mysterious occurred that changed his mind.

As a "Christ-Filled Sybil", Joan possessed the limited ability to perceive many otherwise hidden aspects such as the nature of circumstances, a person's intent or history, or other private aspects. It is probably true that Joan could very well see into the heart of a matter and discern if she was being deceived or not. It is a fact that not much escapes the perceptive ability of someone with well-developed and genuine powers of clairvoyance. So, due to Joan's powers and that ineffable "something" that compelled many people to see something more in her, Joan went from being mocked and shirked to being financially supported and endorsed by Robert. Joan was sent to Chinon under a royal warrant (seal). Robert and others secured Joan a good horse, armor, supplies, and he ordered that an armed party of knights accompany her. This group was composed of some four to six of Robert's trusted knights and squires on the dangerous journey through Burgundian-held territory. The two leading escorts are known to history as Jean de Metz and Bertrand de Poulengy, both of whom survived Joan during the wars and later testified at The Trial of Nullification.

---

[160] The Battle of the Herrings, also called the Battle of Rouvray, was a minor skirmish near the town of Rouvray in France, just north of Orléans, that took place on February 12, 1429 during the siege of Orléans in the Hundred Years' War. The battle occurred as a result of French and Scottish forces, led by Charles of Bourbon and Sir John Stewart of Darnley, to intercept a supply convoy headed for the English army at Orléans. The result was a decisive victory for the English. The name is derived from the barrels of Herrings that were being delivered to the English army.

Some dramatic portrayals of Joan present her as someone who was not in touch with her sense of destiny. This is altogether untrue. Joan was an individual who was deeply in touch with her divine mission and destiny and this is reflected in her comments and leadership. Her confidence, which was firm and apparent, in her mission drove the men forward and led them to victory. Her mission was consistently supported by her miracles, as they were perceived by others, and the special sense of her energy, or being, that compelled loyalty.

So, as history tells us, Joan stayed at a hotel for several days after arriving in Chinon while she awaited a meeting with Charles. She accomplished this first by seeing through a deception that was intended to disprove her by replacing one of Charles's subordinates with his royal cloak. Joan easily located Charles in a group of people as he tried to conceal himself, thus proving she had some measure of genuine spiritual capability that can only be the result of, in medieval terms, the work of God (or the devil if you are in the inquisition or the enemy camp). Charles chose to believe the former. Joan later stated that her spiritual guides helped and directed her to Charles.

She agreed to furnish more proof and she then spoke to the king in private and, although no testimony survives to corroborate it, evidently forbade Charles from revealing certain things so the public, thus we will never know what was discussed. Some have speculated that the information may have been the precise details of prayers that were submitted by Charles on All Saints Day the prior year at his castle on Loches, but this is related only through third-party letters long after Joan's death. We must also remember that, during that period, many of the French were superstitious people, thus someone with Joan's abilities would greatly impress those who were still in touch with the old traditions of divination, nature spirits, visions, and Oracles.

During Joan's first meeting with Charles, she asked for arms, horses, and soldiers and petitioned the King to lead them into battle as the fulfillment of the Maid of Lorraine prophecy. It is interesting that someone with no formal knightly training, as a poor farm woman, so impressed the French nobles at court that one of them gave her a horse and all rallied behind her. It is also revealing that Joan was allowed to handle a lance in the presence of the king without any bodyguard or escort present and was allowed to do so in private. This is highly irregular. It is clear that Joan had earned the king's trust to the highest degree possible as certain protocols that follow discourse with a King, in any country, were disregarded as those of common rank, and even nobles, were never allowed to carry weapons in the presence of any king at the royal court.

"Jeanne then made several requests to the King—amongst others that he would make a gift of his kingdom to the King of Heaven, because the King of Heaven, after this gift, would do for him as He had done for his predecessor, and reinstate him in all his rights. Many other things were said, up to the hour of dinner, which I do not remember. After dinner the King went for a walk; Jeanne coursed before him, lance in hand. Seeing her manage her lance so well I gave her a horse."[161]

So, Joan is granted permission to the lead the army, and a series of smaller miracles, such as they were perceived by others, begin to occur that were clear signs of Joan's direct connection to her "saints" and divine guides. No one understood it, but they believed in it. The proof was always there. A further revelation regarding Joan's mission revealed precisely where to locate the sword of St. Catherine that had been lost and misplaced In Touraine not far from Chinon in the Church of Saint Catherine de Fierbois. This sword was reputed to be the same implement donated to that particular church by Charles Martel "The Hammer" that he carried during his victory over the Moselm Caliphate at the Battle of Poitiers (Tours) in 732AD.

Inquisitors: "How did you know that there was an ancient sword buried in the ground under the rear of the altar of the church of St. Catherine of Fierbois?"

Joan: "I knew the sword was there because my Voices told me so, and I sent to ask that it be given to me to carry in the wars. It seemed to me that it was not very deep in the ground. The clergy of the church caused it to be sought for and dug up; and they polished it, and the rust fell easily off from it."

---

[161] The Retrial of 1456. The English translation of the trial files from 1902. From the book: Jeanne d'Arc Maid of Orléans Deliverer of France. Edited by T. Douglas Murray, Deposition of The Duke d'Alençon.

"This sword was in the earth, all rusty, and there were upon it five crosses, and I knew it by my voices.... I wrote to the prelates of the place that if they please I should have the sword and they sent it to me. It was not very deep underground behind the alter, as it seems to me, but I do not know exactly whether it was before or behind the altar. After this sword was found, the prelates of the place had it rubbed, and at once the rust fell from it without difficulty. There was an arms merchant of Tours who went to seek it, and the prelates of that place gave me a sheath, and those of Tours also, with them, had two sheaths made for me: one of red velvet and the other of cloth-of-gold, and I myself had another made of right strong leather. But when I was captured, it was not that sword which I had. I always wore that sword until I had withdrawn from Saint-Denis after the assault against Paris."[162]

Charles, now sufficiently convinced after Joan's examination at Poitiers by church officials, provided Joan with the support, supplies, an army, and all of the endorsements that she needed to lead the French army to victory at the Siege of Orléans from October 12, 1428, to May 8, 1429. The lifting of the siege at the fortified town of Orléans where thousands of people were starving and unable to defend themselves against a well-trained and experienced army, was located at a critical crossroads on the border between French and English-held territory. Some of the accounts of the retrial state the French captains were unanimous in their opinion that the city could *not* be taken. The defeat of the English at Orléans is a watershed moment that changed the outcome of the war. Had Orléans fallen, the English would have certainly pushed further into France and eventually taken Charles prisoner after laying siege to Chinon.[163] Then, their ambitions may have pushed further into Europe and other nations would have fallen.

There were various predictions made by Joan, and the mysterious occasions marked by Joan's involvement, during the Battle for Orléans and not all of them shall be covered here. However, one occasion, in particular, stands out as a clear connection to Joan's description by Steiner as a

---

[162] From the transcripts of Joan's Trial of 1431, February 26.

[163] The military leader of the English at the siege was a certain John of Lancaster, 1st Duke of Bedford who worked through his subordinate, Thomas Montagu, 4th Earl of Salisbury who was wounded at the siege and died later that year. Together, they laid siege to Orléans. Bedford played an important role during the French-English wars. He later acquired and held Joan in captivity at his estate for a time after purchasing her from the Burgundians after her capture in 1430. He later died in 1435.

"Christ-Filled Sybil"; a seer whose clairvoyance is connected spiritually to the elements of the air (wind), earth, fire (heat), and water.

> "But to reach Orléans it was necessary to sail against the stream, and the wind was altogether contrary. Then Jeanne said to me: "Are you the Bastard of Orléans?" "Yes," I answered; "and I am very glad of your coming!" "Is it you who said I was to come on this side [of the river], and that I should not go direct to the side where Talbot and the English are?" "Yes, and those wiser than I are of the same opinion, for our greater success and safety.
>
> "In God's Name," she then said, "the counsel of My Lord is safer and wiser than yours. You thought to deceive me, and it is yourselves who are deceived, for I bring you better succor (i.e., help, advice, assistance, etc.) than has ever come to any general or town whatsoever—the succor of the King of Heaven. This succor does not come from me, but from God Himself, Who, at the prayers of Saint Louis and Saint Charlemagne, has had compassion on the town of Orléans, and will not suffer the enemy to hold at the same time the Duke and his town!
>
> "At that moment, the wind, being contrary, and thereby preventing the boats going up the river and reaching Orléans, turned all at once and became favorable."[164]

After the victory at Orléans, Joan was regarded as a national hero. Her reputation grew, news of her so-called miracles circulated, and she entered a time when - had she been of weaker character - she may have succumbed to the temptations of pride, vanity, and egotism. But such was Joan...she was impervious to these temptations having purged them from her soul. She was assertive but never vainglorious. She led from the front and adorned herself with accouterments, armor, and a beautiful banner, but not for the sake of vanity. She did so to inspire and rally the people to victory as she was asked to do...

The battles and specific movements of Joan from 1428-1431 will not be explored in detail as it is outside the scope of this work. Much research has

---

[164] The Retrial of 1456. The English translation of the trial files from 1902. From the book: Jeanne d'Arc Maid of Orléans Deliverer of France. Edited by T. Douglas Murray, Deposition of Jean Bastard of Orléans, Count de Dunois.

been done on these topics by conscientious researchers and is available for free on the internet and through printed material. However, perhaps by providing accounts provided by eyewitnesses who knew Joan during these battles and participated in them, we can gather some insights into Joan's activities and character of one whose behavior and activities were enlightened, or broadened, by a form of clairvoyance, and compassion, that was colored by a natural disposition and intuitive knowledge of the battlefield.

What is revealed is that Joan was not simply a figurehead, but rather led directly from the front. She was not one of these would-be leaders who preferred to stand in the background out of harm's why while others fought and died. She led from the front, gave specific orders, received battle wounds, and pushed the men forward to victory. She was highly communicative and active in the relaying of messages to her captains and with Charles VII. On at least one occasion, Joan was required to go to Charles and implore him to continue with the mission when he began to hesitate and vacillate. In other words, she overcome obstacles both within and without and rallied others to continue forward when their will and desire began to wane. This is the mark of a true leader. They have always existed in the world but rarely make it into public life. There are always appointed leaders who find a path to leadership positions through politics, of course, but very few *genuine* leaders.

In some cases, Joan was observed giving soldiers specific orders on where to attack and even stand during the battles. It is quite clear through first-hand accounts from those who participated in these battles that Joan was with the troops continually and guided them on specific battle tactics, places to be, and what to do...as testimonies have proven throughout surviving letters and the Trial of Nullification in 1456. It is due to Joan's unique mission, and her true conviction to Christ's values, that she never harmed anyone.

> "I remember that Jeanne was asked why she always marched with a banner in her hand? "Because," she answered, "I do not wish to use my sword, nor to kill anyone."[165]

---

[165] The Retrial of 1456. The English translation of the trial files from 1902. From the book: Jeanne d'Arc Maid of Orléans Deliverer of France. Edited by T. Douglas Murray, Deposition of Brother Séguin de Séguin Dominican, Professor of Theology, Dean of the Faculty of Theology of Poitiers.

After the victory at Orléans, Joan moved on to the small town of Jargeau that was on the southern bank of the Loire some ten miles east of Orléans. In another demonstration of Joan's Sybil-like powers, testimony was provided at the Trial of Nullification by the Duc (Duke) d'Alencon, a commander in the later phase of the wars who became Joan's close friend after meeting her at Chinon when she first appeared before Charles VII:

> "During the assault on Jargeau Jeanne said to me: "Go back from this place, or that engine"—pointing out an engine of war in the city—"will kill you." I retired and shortly after that very engine did indeed kill the Sieur de Lude in that very place from which she told me to go away. On this account I had great fear, and wondered much at Jeanne's words and how true they came."[166]

> "Joan breathed the will of God into French troops ensuring them their victory saying 'Act, and God will act!' ... a stone hit her on the head... (splitting her helmet in two as she scaled a wall on a ladder), causing her to fall. But driven on by her determination, she got up, and exhorted her companions forward...the French took Jargeau and set off in pursuit of the running English."[167]

The concept of "breathing" new life into someone is a spiritual concept regardless of how modern materialists choose to misuse or misapply the term. In the context of Joan, and in light of Steiner's research, this breath was an energetic impulse that was connected to the Christ. It was something that could be felt and sensed. It invigorated and inspired people.

In reality, while Joan's mission is unusual to be sure, these types of accounts are common in her life as told and recounted by those who knew or came into contact with her in one form or another. In modern times, people have replaced genuine spiritual energy and vision, as it were, and the movement of activity as it surrounds people in a hidden way, with the concept of "luck" or "chance" that are meaningless terms created by people who cannot see or look beyond the veil of the physical world.

---

[166] Ibid. Deposition of The Duke d'Alençon.
[167] Ibid.

As a result, sometimes the line between Joan's spiritual faculties and luck is ambiguous when viewed in a modern context. But for the Frenchman of the 15th century who was fighting alongside Joan, it was self-evident that she was on a genuine divine mission as random events seemed to occur repeatedly when, and where, Joan was involved that benefited the French. In reality, there is no such thing as luck. In life, although only effects are visible in an outer way, human activity is the result of the activities of higher beings, fate, karma, destiny, and free will. It is, therefore, valid to view the events of Joan's battles, in light of Dr. Steiner's insights, as an individual on an official and ordained spiritual mission, as it were.[168] One such event occurred during the critical and perhaps most important rout during the Battle of Patay on June 18, 1429, which is considered by some historians, and the French of the 15th century, to be the proportional response to the disastrous defeat of the French at the Battle of Agincourt in 1415.

At Patay, the English employed the same strategy as they had done at the Battles of Agincourt and Crécy by stacking long-bow archers in the woods behind long wood sharpened poles where they hoped to ambush the French into a charge up the middle of the field on cavalry, thus being annihilated by English archers. This did not come to pass for two reasons; first, the ground was firm at Patay. In Agincourt, the ground was saturated with mud due to heavy rains the night before, thus the French cavalry charged and became entrenched in the mud-sodden field. The French were slaughtered almost to the man.

---

[168] "Until you make the unconscious conscious, it will direct your life and you will call it fate." Carl Jung, The Collected Works of C.G. Jung. In their blindness, many people today refer to the phenomenon of fate in the West as "luck", which is a meaningless and superstitious term that refers to a mysterious, invisible, and unknown power that lands randomly on certain people producing positive or negative outcomes that always favors one over the other.

Jeanne à la bataille de Patay
(Extrait de *Jeanne d'Arc vierge et martyre* par l'abbé Fesch).

The Battle of Patay, 1429.

Second, as was the case with battles and events where Joan is involved, there was an unexplained incident that seemed to be the work of fate or the result of Joan's divine inspired mission. During an attempt to redeploy archers to a hidden location, the English archers were somehow startled by a stag or deer that wandered into their area and thus caused them to reveal their location. It could be that someone yelled or that the archers thought the stag was a French cavalryman, and thus yelled an alarm. Whatever the case, it turned the tide of battle. The French knights hurried and overwhelmed those vulnerable positions and the English were put to flight.

So, a random stag moving across the battlefield caused the English archers to give away their position and thus resulted in a tremendous victory for the French. It was at the Battle of Patay that Joan is remembered for dismounting her horse and tending to the English wounded who lay helplessly dying on the field after the battle.

As the end of 1430 approached, Joan had accomplished a series of astounding victories yet she was ordered to the royal court at Sully Castle where she was kept under observation for the winter months. In the medieval period, armies rarely fought during the winter months and used that time to prepare and rest for the coming spring. Had Charles been an able commander, he would have utilized that time to reequip, heal the army, recruit new soldiers, and prepare for future battles. With Joan waiting anxiously at Sully, he could easily have made a fresh start when the snow melted and continued the task. This did not come to be.

Towards the end of Joan's journey in the field, virtually everyone except a handful of people had abandoned her. Many of the French commanders were ordered to stop aggressive action, thus their soldiers and lancers were held back. During that period, Joan was ordered into the Compiègne area. The continuing political intrigues of the inept rulership of Charles VII hindered Joan's ability to fulfill her mission, thus in the end, there were perhaps some 200-300 fellow knights, soldiers, and supporters who were traveling with her in the spring of 1430. The precise number of those accompanying her is not known.

After the failed Siege of Paris and Charite-sur-Loire, which lasted several months, Jeanne's career is perceived to have begun to wither although in December 1429 Charles VII promoted her and her family to noble status. Regardless, there was a deliberate plan afoot to discredit Joan and remove her from political favor by at least two of Charles's advisors. In 1430, the Duke of Burgundy threatened the regions of Compiègne and Brie, and Jeanne promised Charles she would protect the regions. As confirmed by Dr. Steiner, this was a trap invented by the jealousy of Joan's advisors. Some accountings of Joan's journeys imply and hypothesize that Joan was aware of this reality and went on the mission to Compiègne anyways knowing it was her duty and obligation to do so. Given her strong powers of clairvoyance, it is the author's perspective is that this most likely the case.

> "But we can also point to her death which occurred because all the Luciferic forces of her enemies joined together to bring about her death. Her misadventure in a battle was brought about through the jealousy of the men who were the official leaders, appointed to guide the battle. All the jealousy then came to the fore over the manifestations of spiritual forces and spiritual powers that were made through her."[169]

As it turns out, Charles had made yet another of his many secret agreements with the English or the Burgundians. This time, he agreed to trade off the citizens and town of Compiègne to the Burgundians without the mayor's knowledge or approval. The people of Compiègne refused to acquiesce and held out. It is this fact that leads one to reasonably conclude that the mayor of Compiègne was not involved in a conspiracy to cut Joan

---

[169] Steiner, Rudolf. The Destinies of Individuals and of Nations, Lecture 5. The Nature of the Christ Impulse and the Michaelic Sprit Serving It, Berlin, January 19, 1915.

off on a general retreat to the city walls. However, given the political instabilities of the time, anything is feasible. Historically, some held the mayor of Compiègne personally responsible thus his reputation suffered throughout the remainder of his life. The reality is that Charles and his advisors allowed Joan to walk into a high-risk situation while leading an understrengthed group of lancers and soldiers.

Jeanne was accompanied to Compiègne by her brother Pierre, her loyal squire Jean de Aulon, and a handful of her most loyal supporters. Her numbers were most likely in the hundreds. They should have been in the thousands. The king and the lords abandoned Joan and she was vulnerable to being overwhelmed by a superior force. Charles, it appears, was determined to pursue a path of capitulation that included surrendering his greatest hero and the city of Compiègne to the enemy. It was a disgraceful betrayal.

Regardless of Joan's capture, the citizens refused to surrender and held out for several months until the English finally withdrew. Joan, in her noble spirit, went to Compiègne to defend the citizens knowing the risks. After her capture, Jeanne immediately swore to her captors that she would do nothing to betray Charles VII, even though someone in Joan's position with her powers of clairvoyance, assume she perceived that she had been betrayed, may have had reason to be bitter. Joan was not. This was a part of Joan's path.

> "Then the Maid (Jeanne d'Arc), surpassing the nature of a woman, took on a great force, and took much pain to save her company from defeat, remaining behind as the leader and as the bravest of the troop. But their fortune permitted for the end of her glory and for the last time that she would ever carry arms. An archer, a rough and very sour man, full of much spite because a woman, who so much had been spoken about, should have defeated so many brave men, as she had done, grabbed the edge of her cloth-of-gold doublet, and threw her from her horse flat to the ground."[170]

Thus, Joan's heroic mission in the field came to an end in a disgraceful way. She had accomplished her spiritual task, but her battle was not over. She was left with a personal quest, the substance of which was to face the enemy and be exposed. There would be no withdrawals or retreats. Joan

---

[170] The Description of Joan's capture by Burgundian Georges Chastellain.

was always brave and of a high heart, as was revealed throughout her harrowing journey, thus she faced this impossible situation with faith, heart, endurance, and skill as the enemy mercilessly laid siege to her in a meticulous, corrupted, and malicious manner. She faced this challenge in the spirit of a true knight and hero of the medieval period. Thus, in every sense, Joan's sacrifice and contribution live on…

Above: "Joan captured by the Burgundians at Compiègne". Mural in the Panthéon, Paris, circa 1886–1890.

Joan of Arc's Death at the Stake by Hermann Stilke circa 1843.

"We declare you of right excommunicate and heretic, being stubborn and obstinate in your crimes, excesses and errors; and we pronounce it meet to abandon you to the secular justice as a limb of Satan, infected with the leprosy of heresy, cut off from the Church, in order to prevent the infection of the other members of Christ..."[171]

"Alas! Rouen, I fear me that thou wilt have to suffer for my death." Shortly after she began to cry "Jesus" and to invoke St. Michael; and then she perished in the flame."[172]

After her capture, Joan was moved across several Burgundian and English-held castles until she finally landed in Rouen to stand trial. During the trial, which took place between January 9 and May 30, 1431, Joan passed through a long series of challenges, stresses, assaults, and interrogations. Given Joan's military and political accomplishments, statements, and the nature of her being that seemed to have no fear, yet inspired compassion due to her thoughtful and intelligent disposition, she compelled her persecutors and notary-scribes into a state of confusion and conflict. Those present drifted between a genuine heartfelt appreciation of Joan and absolute hatred. As it was a period of war, her opponents used deception, dishonesty, and manipulation to achieve a verdict that suited their self-interest.

The nature of corruption, which seeks to conceal the truth of things for the sake of posterity and egotism, seeks to create and foster an illusion that casts one in the best possible light despite the low nature of one's intentions. One can see why, in light of the reality of Joan's gifts and abilities and genuine honest nature, that the bishops and inquisitors at her trial were irritated and fearful at the prospect of a simple farm woman, and a "woman" at that, with no education being the bearer, messenger, and

---

[171] The last words as addressed to Joan of Arc on Wednesday, May 30, 1431 prior to her execution.

[172] The English translation of the trial files from 1902. From the book: Jeanne d'Arc Maid of Orléans Deliverer of France. Edited by T. Douglas Murray, Deposition of Maître Guillaume Delachambre Master in Arts and Medicine. Thus, even in death after being condemned on false grounds, Joan lamented for those present, as drawn by their individual destinies who might later suffer, on karmic grounds, because of her martyrdom. This statement carries with it many implications from the perspective of a seer with genuine clairvoyance, including how the effects of injustice can carry forth into others who willingly, or unwillingly, participate in the persecution of a genuine representative of Christ.

herald of the Archangel Michael and the saints who worked on behalf of the Christ when they, as entitled and educated male aristocrats and theologians, surely felt that were the anointed intermediaries for the divine.[173] It is clear that at least some of the bishops and inquisitors envied Joan and held her in high regard. Some even wept on the day of execution.

In reality, a kind of spiritual jealousy can manifest in certain circumstances and that antagonism contributed to the determined and resolute way in which Joan was tried, convicted, and murdered. The English secular membership treated Joan as a hostile enemy of the state. Some persecuted Joan relentlessly while others, who were quickly censored, fled or were driven by force from the proceedings by Bishop Cauchon on threat of death if they resisted or sought to protect and defend Joan in their peculiar fashion.[174] None, however, stood their ground and risked their lives in Joan's defense. Here is an example:

> "One day, when Jeanne was being questioned, Jean de Châtillon spoke in her favor, saying that she was not compelled to reply to the question put to her, or to that effect. This much displeased the Bishop of Beauvais and his following, and there was a great tumult at his words. The Bishop ordered him to be quiet, and to let the Judges speak. On another occasion, when someone was advising

---

[173] Generally speaking, an English or French lord, and peasant, of the 15th century possessed a misogynistic attitude towards women. Women were sometimes regarded as crafty, wily things not to be trusted who inspired men to be deceived. This attitude appears in subtle form in some aspects of the trial. There was a deep and genuine fear of Joan both as a woman and a messenger of the Archangel Michael and the Christ.

[174] An example of one who came to Joan's defense emerges in the behavior of the leading English leader William de Beauchamp, 9th Earl of Warwick who on the one hand was a military leader who waged war against the French. On the other hand, he was compelled to protect Joan on at least two occasions from assaults by English guards. During Joan's incarceration at Castle Philip Augustus, Warwick kept Joan in a tower directly next to his apartments because he was responsible for Joan as her jailor but also so that he could keep a personal eye on her (this included spying on her through a secret room). This kind of deed to protect Joan was unnecessary, and a bit unusual, with the English when incarcerated their political enemies, so it must be considered that Warwick was influenced by Joan in a positive way to some extent as he was an active captain, advisor, and leading political figure of that time under King Henry V and later served as the tutor and regent of his son, Henry VI. Enemies who bore arms against the English throne historically were shown little, if any, compassion and were treated harshly prior to their brutal executions that typically involved torture and humiliation first, such as being drawn and quartered, in a public ceremony.

and directing Jeanne on the question of submission to the Church, the Bishop said, "Hold your tongue, in the devil's name!"[175]

Le jugement de Jeanne d'Arc - Painting by Anthony Serres, 1867

Countless arguments were hurled at Joan over the course of some five months that sought to discredit and manipulate her through skillful and subtle arguments and the art of legal rhetoric; an art that many of the inquisitors had mastered as lawyers and doctors of the church. Joan, who could neither read nor write, had no objective legal representation and the legate assigned to her was a pro-English ecclesiastical representative. The prosecutors sought to continually lure Joan into an admission of guilt, make a false statement, and otherwise discredit herself so they could vindicate their political and financial self-interest.[176] However, Joan's simple faith, wit, remarkable memory, clairvoyance, and the guidance she received from her spiritual guardians always prevailed especially in her darkest moments of fear and suffering. Joan never seemed to hesitate or stumble in any of

---

[175] The Retrial of 1456. The English translation of the trial files from 1902. From the book: Jeanne d'Arc Maid of Orléans Deliverer of France. Edited by T. Douglas Murray, Fourth Examination, 17th December, 1455. Additional statements.

[176] In anthroposophical terms, I would argue that this is a Luciferic attribute (egotism) that uses an Ahrimanic device (cleverness). The art of subtlety as it relates to rationalizing one' self-interest stems from a narcissistic and punitive attitude to lure one into a trap and thus vindicate the accuser by saying that an outcome was, in fact, the fault of he or she who fell into the trap. The trial is thoroughly interwoven with that strategy.

the testimony provided by those who witnessed her during those difficult months. Joan's struggle was amplified by humiliation, deprivation, emotional stress, and the constant threat of execution. In and around Joan's cell were five English guards of the "lowest kind". She had no bed or furniture in her cell towards the end of her journey. The persecutors worked on Joan day and night...

> "The interrogations sometimes lasted three or four hours in the morning; and sometimes difficult and subtle questions arose on the answers, on which she was further examined after dinner for two or three hours. Often, they turned from one question to another, changing about, but, notwithstanding this, she answered prudently, and evinced a wonderful memory, saying often, "I have already answered you on this," and adding, "I refer to the clerks."[177]

> "One day, I went with the Bishop of Beauvais and the Earl of Warwick to the prison where Jeanne was, and we found her in irons. It was said that at night she was fastened with iron chains, but I did not see her so fastened. There was, in the prison, neither bed nor any kind of couch. There were four or five guards of the lowest kind."[178]

However, during the trial, Joan managed to retain something of her sense of humor which is astounding given the circumstances of the moment. The sense of her being a kind of Holy Mother, or Catholic school teacher, manifests from time to time in the transcripts of both the Trial of 1431 and the Trial of Nullification/Rehabilitation. For example:

> "I heard from several, during the Trial, that Jeanne was quite wonderful in her answers, and that she had a remarkable memory; for, on one occasion, when questioned as to a point on which she had answered eight days before, she replied: "I was asked about this eight days ago, and thus replied." Boisguillaume, the other notary, said she had not answered; and, when some of those present declared that what Jeanne said was true, the answers of that day were read: and it was found that Jeanne had spoken right. At this

---

[177] The Retrial of 1456. The English translation of the trial files from 1902. From the book: Jeanne d'Arc Maid of Orléans Deliverer of France. Edited by T. Douglas Murray, Deposition of Manchon, Fourth Examination, 17th December, 1455. Additional statements.
[178] Ibid.

she rejoiced, saying to Boisguillaume that, if he made mistakes again, she would pull his ears!"[179]

And, during her questioning at Poitiers, which was not a criminal investigation but a formal inquiry nonetheless, Joan was not afraid to confront those whom she felt deserved a "pull of the ears".

> "I, in my turn, asked Jeanne what dialect the Voice spoke? "A better one than yours," she replied. I speak the Limousin dialect. "Do you believe in God?" I asked her. "In truth, more than yourself!" she answered."[180]

Thus, we again see evidence of Joan's inherent abilities that someone of her education and background typically would not possess at such a young age without a formal education. It was her intelligence and commentary that convinced so many learned people that she must have been, given the rarity of her inherent capabilities, on a genuine divine mission.

> "I heard from these said Doctors that they had examined her and put many questions, to which she replied with much prudence, as if she had been a trained divine; that they marveled at her answers, and believed that, taking into account her life and conversation, there must have been in her something divine."[181]

The farse that was called a Trial in 1431 demonstrates, in its truest nature, the path of the genuine Christian martyr who follows a spiritual mission that is in alignment with the will and principles of the guiding higher spiritual beings of humanity. That path follows a necessary course that extends beyond egotism and one must endure the low-minded insults of blind and corrupted people. Contrary to those who pursue a public task for power, wealth, self-interest, and vanity, the course charted by genuine spiritual martyrs is quite the opposite. They follow the purified dictates of their conscience and die by the virtue and conviction of the higher principles and values that live within them. While some simply follow their

---

[179] The Retrial of 1456. The English translation of the trial files from 1902. From the book: Jeanne d'Arc Maid of Orléans Deliverer of France. Edited by T. Douglas Murray, Deposition of Pierre Daron Locum Tenens, Deputy to the Bailiff of Rouen.

[180] Ibid. Deposition of Brother Séguin de Séguin Dominican, Professor of Theology, Dean of the Faculty of Theology of Poitiers.

[181] Ibid. Deposition of Maître Jean Barbin Doctor of Laws, King's Advocate.

conscience, Joan was unique in that she was following the direct advice of higher spiritual beings on a genuine mission for the Christ, the Archangel Michael, and the Spiritual Hierarchies. Regardless of the pathway of the information received, genuine spiritual martyrs throughout history have found their way to a painful death as a part of a life task. Some, like Joan, meet painful and traumatic ends in isolation persecuted by those who seek to pursue the lonely and difficult path of egotism and tyranny over others.

This is not the same concept as those who fight for political, economic, or egotistical reasons. Fighting and dying for one's cut, or profit percentage, does not make one a martyr. Countless people throughout history, and in the modern world, are viewed as being martyrs while serving a higher ideal when, in fact, the opposite is the case. In truth, to be a genuine martyr is to sacrifice one's future and give back one's self for a cause that truthfully benefits the welfare and destiny of others. It gives one's self up in service, and life, for a higher cause. Joan was a genuine martyr. She pursued a path that went against her grain, as it were, by leading an army based on the instructions from her spiritual guides that served a higher purpose that benefitted not just the French but the English, Burgundians, Western Europe, and indeed the world.

The soul that became Jeanne d' Arc is an individuality that is deeply connected to the Christ and Michael Impulse and it would be invalid to view her, in exoteric terms, as a simple farm girl who was not aware of the nature of the risks and the importance of the task at hand. Despite her lack of education and inability to write, Joan possessed a highly developed wit, a good heart, a fair mind, a remarkable memory, sincere bravery, a strong will, and a discerning disposition rooted in an innate form of genuine clairvoyance that could pierce the veil of the outer world, as it were. She cherished the dignity of the human being and maintained a sense of honor. She held her family, the piety of others, the Christ, the Angels, and the church in the highest regard as sacred and living principles to be cherished, advocated, and defended.

The forces that Joan was battling, in corruption, decadence, deception, and the lower elements of the human soul, also caused Jeanne to meet her destiny. Steiner tells us that these were the triumph of Luciferic forces, having interrupted her mission but not before it could be completed, that worked through her antagonists. Joan only undertook her path onto the battlefield because her spiritual guides insisted upon it as a mission that would serve the destiny of the world through France. Perhaps, all she knew was that she was serving a higher purpose and did not understand the global scope and nature of her mission. Steiner implies in his lectures that this was the case. Whatever the truth may be, Joan reluctantly pursued the path of war as she was naturally predisposed to a life of peace, the church, the farm, and home. Before she began her journey to Chinon, Joan was simply Jeanne of Domrémy who was compelled to heed the advice of her spiritual guides. By the time she reached Chinon, she was petitioning the King to lead his armies into battle. She was, and almost everyone accepted her as such in the French court and the army, the fulfillment of the Maid of Lorraine prophecy that was passed down through the legends of Merlin.

Before the beginning of her public mission in 1429, as she stated to others, Joan knew that she would survive only one year thus she was aware of her destiny. She was conscious of the implications of her mission knowing that it would only last a predefined period of time. During her imprisonment at Rouen, Joan consciously confronted and accepted the reality of her destiny to its fullest extent. Joan was led to the gallows by an armed English company of 80 men. What a dramatic and ridiculous show of force by the English nation! Surely, it was not until being led to the scaffold by this honor guard of destiny to be burned alive that the magnitude of her sacrifice manifested in physical terms with the fire in front of her.

> "She was taken to the place of execution by a large number of soldiers—nearly fourscore. After the ecclesiastical sentence had been pronounced, and Jeanne given up, she was taken over to the Bailly, there present, who, without any consultation or sentence, made a sign with his hand, saying: "Take her away! Take her away!"[182]

Rudolf Steiner reveals that it is only in death that one truly comprehends and perceives the journey of life. Despite her powers of clairvoyance, and the surety of the voices of her spiritual guides, the pain of the pathway through the membrane of a painful death is traumatic. Surely this was the case with Joan as she approached the end seeing that her path was fixed. One can, after all, imagine the pain of death, but no one knows what it

---

[182] The Retrial of 1456. The English translation of the trial files from 1902. From the book: Jeanne d'Arc Maid of Orléans Deliverer of France. Edited by T. Douglas Murray, Deposition of Manchon, Third Examination 8th May, 1452. A "score" is 20.

feels like until one passes through it. Nonetheless, regardless of the certainty of death, one holds out hope not knowing for sure where the path is going to end until it appears solidified as an indisputable and irrevocable fact. Despite this reality, however, while some who have been led to the gallows under false pretenses express bitterness and opposition to the end, Joan's approach was quite different. She forgave, blessed, and even made it a point to spiritually encourage others who were her bitterest enemies.

Conversions took place through Joan. It happened on several occasions, and as stated previously, many were transformed by Joan simply through her glance, disposition, or otherwise hidden ways. This was the manifestation of the Christ working through her.

> "She also most humbly begged all manner of people, of whatever condition or rank they might be, and whether of her party or not, for their pardon and asked them kindly to pray for her, at the same time pardoning them for any harm they had done her. This she continued to do for a very long time, perhaps for half an hour and until the end. The judges who were present, and even several of the English, were moved by this to great tears and weeping, and indeed several of these same English, recognized God's hand and made professions of faith when they saw her make so remarkable an end."[183]

> "When Jeanne saw that they were setting fire to the pile, she began to say, with a loud voice, "Jesus!" and constantly, to the end, she cried, "Jesus!"[184]

> "On this same occasion, the Bishop of Beauvais wept. A certain Englishman, a soldier, who hated her greatly, had sworn to bring a faggot for the stake. When he did so, and heard Jeanne calling on the name of Jesus in her last moments, he was stupefied, and, as it were, in an ecstasy at the spectacle: his companions took him and led him away to a neighboring tavern. After refreshment, he revived. In the afternoon, the same Englishman confessed, in my presence,

---

[183] The English translation of the trial files from 1902. From the book: Jeanne d'Arc Maid of Orléans Deliverer of France. Edited by T. Douglas Murray, Deposition of Deposition of Jean Massieu.

[184] Ibid. Deposition of Jean Ricquier Priest, Chaplain in the Cathedral of Rouen, and Curé of the Church at Hendicourt.

to a Brother of the Order of Saint Dominic, that he had gravely erred, and that he repented of what he had done against Jeanne. He held her to be a good woman, for he had seen the spirit departing from her, as it were a white dove, going away from France.

"In the afternoon of the same day, the executioner came to the Convent of the Dominicans, saying to them and to Brother Martin Ladvenu, that he feared he was damned because he had burnt a saint."[185]

So, we see from this testimony that the executioner was definitively transformed by Joan and so taken by it that he had to be consoled by his colleagues. Is it possible that Pierre Cauchon, Bishop of Beauvais, actually wept despite all of his callousness and hatred towards Joan? Is it possible that he too was transformed by the Christ working through Joan and regretted his actions?

The attitude and disposition of Joan, as manifested purely from the transformed soul, as a victim of the most heinous lies, deceptions, and criminal behavior, reveals one who has been truly permeated by the Christ. Joan pursued her task to the best of her ability, succeeded, and pursued the task of her mission despite countless obstacles, ridicule, and insults of the lowest nature.

"Jeanne had, at the end, so great contrition and such beautiful penitence that it was a thing to be admired, saying such pitiful, devout, and Catholic words, that those who saw her in great numbers wept, and that the Cardinal of England and many other English were forced to weep and to feel compassion.

"As I was near her at the end, the poor woman besought and humbly begged me to go into the Church nearby and bring her the Cross, to hold it upright on high before her eyes until the moment of death, so that the Cross on which God was hanging might be in life continually before her eyes.

---

[185] The Retrial of 1456. The English translation of the trial files from 1902. From the book: Jeanne d'Arc Maid of Orléans Deliverer of France. Edited by T. Douglas Murray, Deposition of Third Examination, May 9th, 1452.

"Being in the flames, she ceased not to call in a loud voice the Holy Name of Jesus, imploring and invoking without ceasing the aid of the Saints in Paradise; again, what is more, in giving up the ghost and bending her head, she uttered the Name of Jesus as a sign that she was fervent in the Faith of God, just as we read of Saint Ignatius and of many other Martyrs.

Joan was not just "the Maid". Joan is "Our Maid". No one owns Joan in the sense of possession but as an homage to her sacrifice, she is, in a sense, connected to us and we to her. As Joan's task was a global one, and not just a regional or local one, it is perhaps more apt and fitting to address Joan in this way as a guide and leader who gave her life for the world in the spirit of the Christ and the Archangel Michael who led her on a noble mission on behalf of humanity.

Joan's quality of soul, which was transformed by the Christ, is a consistent aspect of all of those who have taken the Christ into their heart and souls and seek to serve a mission on behalf of humanity just as the Christ did and those who serve His mission. It is a core aspect of those spiritual leaders who have come to lead humanity throughout history and shall do so into the future.

"Immediately after the execution, the executioner came to me and to my companion, Brother Martin Ladvenu, stricken and moved with a marvelous repentance and terrible contrition, quite desperate and fearing never to obtain pardon and indulgence from God for what he had done to this holy woman. And the executioner said and affirmed that, notwithstanding the oil, the sulfur, and the charcoal which he had applied to the entrails and heart of the said Jeanne, in no way had he been able to burn them up, nor reduce to cinders either the entrails or the heart, at which he was much astonished, as a most evident miracle."[186]

Thus, according to one first-hand account, Joan's heart would not, and did not, burn and was left in the smoldering ashes after the debacle had finally concluded...or was it...

---

[186] The Retrial of 1456. The English translation of the trial files from 1902. From the book: Jeanne d'Arc Maid of Orléans Deliverer of France. Edited by T. Douglas Murray, Deposition of Brother Ysambard De La Pierre of the Order of Saint Dominic, of the Convent at Rouen.

Chapter 8: Through the Spiritual Eye of the Author

> "At the end of the sermon the sentence was pronounced...Jeanne began to make many pious exclamations and lamentations...hereupon I left, not wishing to see the burning of Jeanne. I saw many of the bystanders weeping."[187]

Based on the author's visions and clairvoyance, which have gradually unfolded over time through meditation, dreams, and psychic recall, I have experienced certain memories as images characterized by a clairvoyant form of "knowing" regarding certain aspects of Joan's life. These psychic flashes are revived memories perceived, perhaps, through the Akashic Records. As I have perceived and discerned, these memories are based on a person who was connected to Joan of Arc. During that prior lifetime, this person lived as a French squire, soldier, and lancer who fought alongside Joan and was acquainted with her to a limited extent. The following description is based on my observations of that event attained through a limited and budding form of spiritual vision. In an effort to be as transparent as possible, I relay only what I have seen and perceived through my limited clairvoyance.

During the final day of Joan's life on May 30, 1431, she was led before a small crowd of commoners and villagers who had come to witness her final moments. Some came out of morbid curiosity while others came out of a deep and genuine sympathy for the Maid and to be with her in her final moments. May 30 was an overcast day. Rouen, at that time, was not the well-manicured city that it is today or as is sometimes portrayed in art with vivid colors.[188] It was a place of some infrastructure and civility, especially compared to the rural areas of France at that time, but the majority of the town as revealed through my intuition appeared to be constructed of simple one, two, and three-story buildings. The roads and pathways were not paved.

---

[187] The English translation of the trial files from 1902. From the book: Jeanne d'Arc Maid of Orléans Deliverer of France. Edited by T. Douglas Murray, Deposition of Jean de Mailly the Reverend Father in God, the Lord, Bishop of Noyon.

[188] The city of Rouen fell to King Henry V 1in 1419 after a six-month siege. Historians today speculate that approximately 50% of the population died of starvation, wounds, and disease before it fell.

There were no more than 20-30 or so commoners present. There was a pit dug approximately three feet deep with a stake emerging from it over where a platform was erected constructed of wooden beams and planks. It was not a large platform. Behind the Maid and to the left (with a perspective that is facing Joan), was a viewing platform that stood about three feet above the ground with two steps leading up to it on either side. This formal area was made for the prosecutors and legates that consisted of the secular and church representatives. The official stand had an awning above it. Thus, the legates were protected from the elements. There were, in fact, only about ten people present in the official entourage.

To the right and behind the scaffold (Joan's hands were bound behind a single wooden pole) was a single poorly constructed set of wood bleachers that stood about two tiers high and ran down the side of a two-story building that was about 25 feet long. There was no awning on that construction, thus the people were exposed to the weather. Therefore, the English and Church prosecutors sat behind Joan to the left while on the right (facing Joan) the common-folk sat on or stood near a two-tier bleacher section. Some of the spectators stood erect while others sat. Contrary to some stories that have been told over the years, there were not thousands or even hundreds of people present. It was a small group of people. Facing Joan was an open area with no bleachers, seats, or people. No one was allowed to stand or observe Joan from that perspective for some reason. It was a small courtyard. It appears that the 80 or so men, per the testimony of the Trial of Nullification, that led Joan into the courtyard were not allowed to remain in the courtyard as they were not present.

There were only two guards in armor casually standing before an open gateway that was, perhaps, 20 feet in diameter that led to the courtyard facing Joan. The entire area backed up to the viewing stands that created a semi-circle around Joan. The area was, perhaps, some 100 feet or so in diameter from one side to the other. The officials, in true cowardly fashion, were not forced to look at Joan directly during her execution and therefore were not compelled to experience her anguish and suffering. To enter the courtyard, one had to enter through the front gate that directly faced Joan. It was the only entryway, from what I could see. The peasants and observes who came to the execution entered through that gate.

Such was the case with a young male in his mid-20's who eventually found his way into the courtyard in an anonymous fashion after the majority of onlookers had already arrived. He was late and had been hurrying to get there in time. He wore a brown cloak and kept a hood over his head to keep his identity obscured. As he passed through the gate, the two guards took no heed of him and hardly noticed his presence. They were too preoccupied and kept giving each other worrisome glances and appeared to be very distracted...

There, as this young man approached cautiously and slowly, he saw Joan bound to a wooden beam on the platform clothed in an off grey and white robe. He was horrified to see Joan bound to a pole in a public ceremony. She looked fatigued. He gazed at Joan, with tears swelling in his eyes, and made his way to the right side of the courtyard where he stood anonymously in the corner. There, he stared intently at Joan from underneath the lid of his hood hoping to make eye contact with her as she stared off into the distance, her eyes set on the horizon, and paid no attention to those around her.

Finally, at long last, Joan's eyes settled on the young man for a few brief moments. He was relieved to have made eye contact with her. She gave him a brief acknowledgment as if to say that she was glad that at least one person that she knew, or was acquainted with, had come. As far as the man could discern, there were no others that he recognized from the campaigns with Joan. Joan's eyes returned to the horizon and set her mind upwards to the world to which she was going. She appeared to turn within herself and blocked everything out of view. The man's heart shrieked in agony knowing there was nothing that he could do to prevent Joan's death...

The night before Joan's execution, the young man had found himself in a quandary. He had been on the run for some time and had taken up a temporary residence deep in the forest with three poor French monks who agreed to let the young man board with them. One of them, perhaps, was a brother or cousin. There, they shared a small two-room cabin with bunk beds, a fireplace, and one table. The group of men got along well and behaved like a family. Before retiring to the top bunk as the night approached, one of the older monks turned and addressed the young man briefly.

"Are you going tomorrow?"
In tears, the man replied "I am not sure. No."
"You should go."[189]

The young man took heed of the advice, climbed into the top bunk, and laid down to sleep. He did not sleep well and awoke abruptly before dawn. With dire urgency, the young man hurried out of the house as the sun was breaking and headed off into the forest on his way to Rouen. His heart was leaping out of his chest with emotion that, for some reason, he had to be with the Maid one last time regardless of the risk to himself.

That prior year, the young man had been a member of Joan's extended entourage and was frequently seen in the group that was closest to Joan. He, along with several other pages, squires, heralds, monks, and soldiers followed Joan closely while she was on the march and especially when she went into battle. He often rode a horse behind Joan some 5-6 tiers back and always kept an eye on her. He behaved as a kind of bodyguard although he carried no such formal title. Joan had many bodyguards who made it their personal responsibility to protect her. Joan was regarded as a talisman and thus, to be close to Joan was both an honor and a sure sign of good fortune. The army, when it marched, did so in rows of two or three horses. The foot soldiers marched behind the cavalry. Joan always marched in the vanguard or center body of the army in the front row. Thus, the young man, when on the march, always had a clear view of Joan from behind. She sometimes wore a white cape that matched the color of her banner. She wore bright silver armor and appeared as a kind of light on the battlefield. She was easily discernable from great distances.

The young man was with her during most of the sieges and battles, if not all, during the years 1429 and 1430. Joan recognized him at the execution as he had been with her during some of the most stressful moments of the battles. He did not have a personal relationship with Joan, as it were, but she knew of him and he was one of the many soldiers who often followed Joan, asked her for advice, and generally sought simply to be in close vicinity to her. In one instance, it appears that Joan had dismounted from her horse on the field after a battle to tend after a wounded man.[190] At

---

[189] The men would have spoken French. I perceived it in English, which is the only language that the author fluently speaks.
[190] Through historical research, I believe this was the Battle of Patay when Joan was tending to wounded English soldiers on the field.

that moment, the young man charged a wounded English soldier who appeared to be attempting to lunge at Joan. He may have simply been reaching out for compassion, but it was difficult to discern. The charge was so quick and aggressive that Joan gave the young man a worrisome glance, then smiled as she processed what had happened. The young man never forgot that smile of approval from the Maid. He was endeared to her in a personal and protective way from that moment forward...just like so many people were.

During the ambush at Compiègne, the young man was one of those who escaped and managed to make his way into hiding. He moved between the homes of sympathizers, family members, monks, and anyone with whom he could find a place to board. He did not have any money, so he was a virtual vagabond. Sometimes, he slept in the open air because it made him feel like he was back on campaign again. Since Joan's capture, the man had been in a state of perpetual fear, worry, sadness, and anger over her capture and the circumstances of her trial. He also worried for his own life. Knowing Joan's special deeds personally, he spent much time contemplating how Joan, as a divine messenger, could ever be caught after so many victories.

So, on the morning of Joan's execution, the young soldier arrived late to Rouen. At least he could rest now knowing that he had made it to see Joan one last time. Or could he? As the papal and secular officials entered the vestibule, or viewing stand, the leader of the group was adorned in a red velvet cape. The leader of the legates, an old and frail man, ordered and peopled quickly obey. All of the other officials kept their heads bowed in genuflection to him. He possessed a glare of evil and hatred, and his eyes resonated with compassionless apathy. He stopped, perused the crowd slowly and examined each person, and then returned his glare to Joan. Thankfully, his eyes did not fall on the young man for very long. The young man was very worried that he would be recognized having fought so close to Joan on several occasions. But no one recognized him...

The fire that consumed Joan, and the experience of that traumatic event as Joan wept and screamed in agony, brought tears to everyone's eyes. Some of the English guards and ecclesiastical legates could not bear to watch the execution.[191] Were they worried that a lightning bolt from heaven would strike them down? Within his heart, the young man nearly screamed in

---

[191] Eyewitness accounts reveal that many turned away, left the area, or wept openly.

agony over the horror of the experience. Nonetheless, he stayed with Joan to the end...

Thus, the smoldering ashes were all that remained. As the smoke cleared, the papal and secular legates made their way back into a house, or building, that was attached to the viewing stand. No one made an effort to look at anyone any further and simply followed the man, who was Bishop Cauchon, away from the courtyard. Everyone was dazed and in a state of shock including the English guards who appeared to be disoriented.

Suddenly, the young man was overcome with an urge to step forward and look into the pit as an English soldier left the courtyard who had, just moments before, been looking at the remains and fiddling with something. So, the young man took a step forward to glance into the firepit as the English soldier wandered off to speak with someone. Perhaps there was something left? One of Joan's rings or a garment? Something that the young man could keep in honor of her memory?

Shuffling the ashes around, the young man saw something indeed. He sifted through the ashes, even though they were hot, grabbed whatever it was, and quickly dashed out of the ring in a very controlled, if assertive, manner. He turned around as he walked through the gate to see that the bishop had, in fact, returned and was watching the young man with some interest. The English guards, again, took no notice of the young man as he made his way down the street and out of Rouen.

Some time passed, and the young man eventually made his way into a forest area to the West outside of Rouen. There, he paused from fatigue to see what he had recovered. Behold, it was her heart. Joan's heart had not burned. In shock, he openly wept for a time, then took the heart and buried it next to a tree. He buried it deep in the ground so that no one would ever find it. As the young man arose to depart the area, the sound of horses was heard. They were looking for him. He ran deeper into the woods and tried to find a hiding place, but all in vain. There was an interrogation and some resistance, but the man was murdered. He, did not, however, reveal the location or existence of what he had found...[192]

---

[192] History also reveals that the officials returned to the podium and decided to conduct a second, and perhaps even a third, burning probably because of this incident as described here. They subsequently took Joan's remains and ashes and dumped them into a nearby river.

There is a legend that has been passed down over the centuries by those who were at Joan's execution who stated that her heart never burned. What has been lost to history, and is now known, is that there was one who found Joan's heart in the ashes and removed it from the firepit immediately after her execution while the ashes were still hot, as it were. The legend is a historical reality that can only be viewed in a spiritual context. Joan's heart was discovered and taken out of the ashes in Rouen where it was given a natural burial by someone who knew and loved her as a friend and a leader. Today this location is a secret place known only to the initiates, and those who can pierce the veil, as it were, who choose to venture there and remember Joan's life, deeds, and martyrdom...[193]

> "And she did not seem to come from any land, but rather she seemed as one sent from Heaven to support our failing France in her arms... O worthy virgin, worthy of all glory, all praise, worthy of divine honors! O honor of the kingdom, O light of the lily; thou art the light, thou art the glory, not only of the French, but of all Christians! Let Troy no longer rejoice in the memory of Hector; let Greece no longer triumph with her Alexander, nor Africa with her Hannibal; let Italy no longer take pride in her Caesar and other great captains of Rome. And thou, France, even though thou hast no lack of other heroes in the past, be content with the Maid; France, thou mayst dare be proud and enter in the lists with the other nations for military glory, and even, we may very well say, place the Maid above all others."[194]

"I am he that liveth, and was dead; and, behold, I am alive...Amen..."[195]

---

[193] This was perceived by way of individual clairvoyance gradually over time and later confirmed through the author's spiritual guardians.

[194] Barrett, W.P., The Trial of Jeanne D'Arc, translated into English, From the Original Latin and French Documents, Published 1932. This is an abridged quote from a letter written during that time from secretary Alain Chartie to Charles VII.

[195] King James Version, Holy Bible, Revelation 1:18

Chapter 9: A Knight of the Holy Grail

The mystery of Joan's mission and martyrdom, from a perspective of the spiritual sciences, is far more encompassing than has been envisaged by theologians, historical researchers, and perhaps most spiritual researchers up to the moment of the publication of Dr. Steiner's insights in the early 20th century. It is something that cannot be grasped without a deeper and committed study especially if one is accustomed to a surface-level observation. Even approaching Joan's life as a divinely inspired saint in a purely religious context, without any knowledge of the true circumstances of the 15th century, falls short.

Dr. Steiner, through his life's efforts, brings meager researchers, such as the author, who are approaching the mysteries, including the mystery of Joan's mission, for the first time much closer to the significance of Joan's life as it relates to broader transformative impulses that were destined to occur in the 15th century but could not be fulfilled without Joan's, and many others, direct involvement. In reality, Joan was but one team member of a broader group who was helping to ensure that an impulse from the spiritual worlds, through the Christ, was brought forth as a global spiritual impulse into humanity. The great spiritual leaders of humanity worked collaboratively with the Spiritual Hierarchies to facilitate this transformational impulse. Joan took on a public task that led to her that culminated with Joan's genuine and painful martyrdom at Rouen in 1431.

So, to comprehend this deeper mystery, one must consider the following facts. First, over long cycles of time, and only repeated lifetimes, souls are prepared and come forth by destiny to lead missions in the world on behalf of the Spiritual Hierarchies. Joan, as a part of this plan, took on a public role that resulted in her death. Others, including the great leading initiate Christian Rosenkreutz, have also made sacrifices to bring forth the foundation upon which the future transformation of humanity could occur in accordance with the divine plan.

The spiritual fire that reverberates in the heart and the soul resonates forever in any person who shares the struggle, mission, and spirit of Jeanne D'Arc. As one's view expands after reviewing the spiritual reality of Joan's mission, in light of Steiner's observations, it becomes very clear that many people, and divine guides, were involved in her life. Joan, however, can be viewed from a variety of perspectives. Like Christ-Jesus, one does not need to know all of the profound and existential nuances of the great spiritual mission that He served to love, appreciate, and take into one's soul the reality of the mission that brought forth by the redeemer of humanity and how that mission, and love, bonds people and the universe together. It can be felt in the heart and the soul but a true understanding of the history and operative reality, as it were, behind the realities of the Christ, and Joan, remains hidden if we confine a study to the surface.

As Steiner reveals, the Christ and the Archangel Michael worked through Joan in an inner and spiritual representative, and vehicle, to help fulfill a critical and global mission here on earth. It is only by way of the true spiritual facts gathered through genuine spiritual science and research that something of the true nature of Joan's global mission has been uncovered and can thus be appreciated as a global task and not just a regional or cultural one. The demand of our time, in light of the regency of the Archangel Michael that began in 1879, is to approach the spiritual worlds based on objectivity, sound thinking, and facts. This can be best accomplished only by learning from the genuine spiritual leaders of our age, in this case, Rudolf Steiner and others who came before and after him, who learned how to pierce the veil of genuine spiritual-historical research thus bringing insights, methods, and best practices to the rest of us. As a result, we also learn how to form a bridge to the spiritual worlds. This task was, and is, accomplished in the spirit of sacrifice, love, knowledge, truth, and human transformation. This is a quest for the Holy Grail.

Joan became a genuine martyr who emerged from obscurity out of the French countryside led by the path of karma, destiny, the needs of the age in which humanity was passing through, and a broader mission for humanity. She carried within her the spirit of the Christ that was imbued in the very heart of her being before being born as a fulfillment and a quest to bring the Christ impulse to humanity in the 15th century through a fresh spiritual impulse for humanity that would compel the activity of human beings in new directions.

As Steiner reveals, Joan carried Christ's forces into the world through her task. This is not an empty allegorical or symbolic statement that suggests that Joan was simply sympathetic to Christ's mission or theology as modern theologians might suggest. No, there is a real living spiritual aspect, through the Christ living within Joan, that others lacked. Dr. Steiner reveals that Joan was literally carrying the being of the Christ, as a living imprint, in her soul where it remains for all time. Receiving the living Christ within our souls, which is a possibility for all people when they are sufficiently prepared for it, is a path that all human beings can achieve if they choose to pursue it.

As discussed throughout this work, the necessity for this intervention that led to Joan's martyrdom was the result of the progression of the movements of peoples and cultures over time and the opposing forces were able to influence things in a corrupted way. This progression began far, far back in human history and reached, in a cultural sense, a certain apex in the West within the "She-Wolf" of the Roman empire. The Romans represented a low point when imperialistic influences reached a certain apex. Steiner reveals that it was at the darkest moment of human history, in 30AD when the Christ entered into the world and brought the eternal light of His transformational impulse. It is feasible, and probable, that the cultural-spiritual source points that led to the crisis of the 15th century and heightened imperialism that threatened Europe and the world most likely began much earlier in history by way of the same forces that led to the Trojan War in 1200BC.[196]

To offset the outcome of England's imperialistic forces that were threatening France, and thus Europe, at that time required the intercession of the Spiritual Hierarchies who worked through a divine messenger as the bearer of a certain task. That person was Joan of Arc. England and France had to be separated to truly become what they were destined, and hoped, to become as a people. Either country has brought unique cultural influences into the world and those impulses can be traced throughout modern history in a myriad of ways. With the martyrdom of Joan and the fulfillment of her task at the political and national level, the individual Folk Spirits of France, England, and indeed all of Europe had a proper path by which their cultural influences could be brought into the world and thus, it occurred.

So, interwoven with Joan's critical effort was the delivery and integration of a new aspect of human consciousness brought forth to humanity, and as

---

[196] Refer to The Gospel of Hellas, The Mission of Ancient Greece and the Advent of Christ by Friedrich Hiebel as well as Steiner's lecture cycle Greek and Germanic Mythology in the Light of Esotericism, Lecture 4, The Trojan War, Berlin, October 28, 1904 for an overview of the transition that occurred for human consciousness through the event of the Trojan War and the cultural impulse of the Greek civilization.

described by Steiner, as the Consciousness or Spiritual soul. This is tied to yet a third aspect of Joan's mission that is connected to the great initiate and spiritual leader Christian Rosenkreutz of which Joan's task is a part. This connection, as revealed by the Grail Triptych created by Anna May at the request of Rudolf Steiner and destroyed during World War 2. However, a color picture was taken before it was lost. This image, when viewed in light of Spiritual Science, directly links to Joan to the mystery of Christian Rosenkreutz mission for humanity in the 13th century (Steiner reveals the year was 1250AD) which is a fulfillment of the Grail Impulse who henceforth brought the Rose Cross, and Rosicrucianism, to humanity.

Below: The Grail Triptych by artist Anna May as commissioned by Rudolf Steiner. This magnificent image of the Grail journey was destroyed in Hamburg during World War 2.[197]

[197] Refer to Adrian Andersen's book <u>Rudolf Steiner's Esoteric Christianity in the Grail painting by Anna May: Contemplating the sacred in Rosicrucian Christianity</u>, 2017. Larger images are available on the internet and the author's website.

Below: The right section of the painting shows Joan as a guardian, and member, perhaps, of the Brotherhood of the Holy Grail. The 12 shown here are the 12 Leading Initiates of the world. There are 13 figures present. Here, the 12 are overseeing the spiritual initiation of Christian Rosenkreuz that occurred in the mid-13th century. While Joan served a task connected with the mission of C.R. in the 15th century, the nature of the true role of Joan's is a task is one that shall continue.

Interwoven with Joan's mission to enable and protect the introduction of the Consciousness Soul element into the human being per the will of the Spiritual Hierarchies and is just now reaching its fullest expression across the globe, is the hidden quest for the Holy Grail. The quest for the Holy Grail, which is interwoven with the mission of Christian Rosenkreutz in the modern age, has been hidden from humanity over the centuries and it was not until the 20th century that the background, sacrifices, and role of this leader were revealed in such a way that people could begin to approach these great mysteries. Dr. Steiner provides deep insights into the history and sacrifices of this Great Initiate, Christian Rosenkreutz, and those who work alongside him on a broader mission for humanity. It is clear, and self-evident, from the painting done by Anna May that Joan has a direct link and connection to not just the introduction of a new impulse into humanity in the 15th century as brought to us by the Christ, the Archangel Michael, and the Spiritual Hierarchies, but also to the mission of Christian Rosenkreutz and the Grail Impulse. [198]

Steiner reveals that the Holy Grail is a deep mystery that true Rosicrucianism brings to humanity. It was a part of his task to bring knowledge of what the Holy Grail is and how it works within the ongoing transformation of the human being. Many stories and studies of the Grail have come forth over the centuries but most deal with superstitions or veiled stories that conceal deeper esoteric truths behind them. It is not the task of this book to provide a detailed review of the Grail with all of its nuances, aspects, and elements.[199] So, let us refer to a partial description of the Holy Grail as quoted by a high initiate:

> "The external expression for the ego is the blood. That is a great secret, but there have always been human beings who were acquainted with it and who were aware of the fact that copies of the ego of Jesus of Nazareth are present in the spiritual world. And since the Event of Golgotha, there have always been human beings through the centuries who had to see to it that humanity matured

---

[198] The deeper significance of this great initiate's mission is outside of the scope of this work and yet is intimately connected to it as it resonates within Joan's mission. Steiner delivered many lectures on this individual's mission. For example, refer to the lecture cycle by Rudolf Steiner called Esoteric Christianity and the Mission of Christian Rosenkreutz and Esoteric Christianity. Refer to Steiner's body of knowledge available online and for free (voluntary donations) on www.rsarchive.org.

[199] Nor is the author qualified.

slowly to the point where some individuals could accept copies of the ego of Jesus Christ... A secret way had to be found to preserve this ego (or "I") in a silent, deep Mystery until the time when a suitable moment for its use would be at hand. To preserve this secret, a brotherhood of initiates was formed: The Brotherhood of the Holy Grail. This brotherhood goes back to the time when, as is reported, its founder took the chalice that Christ Jesus had used at the Last Supper and collected in it the blood that dripped from the wounds of the Savior when He was hanging on the cross. This founder of the brotherhood collected the blood of Christ Jesus, the expression and copy of His ego, in the chalice that is called the Holy Grail. It was kept in a holy place — in the brotherhood — that through its institution and initiation rites comprised the Brothers of the Holy Grail.

"Today the time has come when these secrets can be revealed because the hearts of human beings can become ripened through spiritual life to an extent where they elevate themselves to an understanding of this great mystery. If Spiritual Science can kindle souls so that they warm up to an engaged and lively understanding of such mysteries, these very souls will become mature enough, through casting a glance at that Holy Grail, to get to know the mystery of the Christ-Ego — the eternal ego into which any human ego can be transformed. This mystery is a reality. All that people have to do is to follow the call by Spiritual Science to understand this mystery as a given fact so that they can receive the Christ-Ego at the mere sight of the Holy Grail. To accomplish this, it is necessary only that one understand and accept these happenings as fact."[200]

Thus, in light of the description of the Holy Grail by Dr. Steiner, each human being can prepare one's self gradually over time to receive an "ego", "imprint", or "copy" of the living Christ as a spiritual and inner transformative event having purged one's lower impulses and vanquished the dragons of one's lower nature. From Dr. Steiner's descriptions, Joan of Arc had achieved this when he reveals that Joan took on an imprint of the Christ before being born in a form of spiritual initiation that he refers to as "natural initiation". It is this link that allows a spiritual researcher to

---

[200] Steiner, Rudolf. The Principle of Spiritual Economy, Lecture VIII, Cologne, Easter Sunday, April 11, 1909, Series GA209. Refer to Steiner's works to explore the great mystery of the Holy Grail.

conclude, based on the facts as revealed by Dr. Steiner, that Joan of Arc was, and is, a carrier of the Christ within her soul being as a genuine Knight, and Representative, of the Holy Grail.

Chapter 10: Final Thoughts

In light of the facts, testimony, and letters brought forth by historical records and the genuine spiritual research of Rudolf Steiner, it is clear and self-evident that the life and mission of Joan of Arc extends far beyond the political and social element in the modern sense. In the life and individuality of Joan, we observe an individual who brought forth a broader task for humanity working from an inherited form of clairvoyance, her wits, conviction, bravery, and the guidance of her spiritual guardians. The real and living power of the Christ worked through Joan on behalf of a broader and global spiritual impulse for humanity.

The Christ is actively at work across the breadth of human activity and He chooses individuals and messengers to assist Him, in both physical and spiritual forms, to act in decisive ways and points in time based on the conditions and needs of a given moment. Sometimes, as was the case with Joan, a crisis emerges driven by the opposing beings of the cosmos who work against the right and appropriate progress of humanity's ongoing spiritual transformation. The force, or impulse, that was imparted into Joan's spirit and soul occurred in a most peculiar way as Dr. Steiner reveals. Before her birth on January 6, as revealed and confirmed by Rudolf Steiner, Christ's cosmic mission was imbued within Joan's soul over two weeks from Christmas to the Epiphany.

Plans are made for tasks of this significance far, far in advance. The soul of Joan was gradually prepared for her incarnation, as Joan, over time. Thus, we see a broader perspective emerge. Not only did the Joan-soul have to reckon with the necessary chasm of amnesia that necessarily follows each soul that crosses the gulf between the spiritual and physical worlds as it reincarnates and is forced to drink from the river of forgetfulness, she went into her incarnation knowing that she would meet a painful and gruesome end if, and only if, she was able to accomplish her mission.[201]

---

[201] Many ancient Greeks, as documented by Plato, believed that souls were forced to drink from the "River of Forgetfulness" before being reincarnated so they would not remember their past-lives as they had not earned the knowledge, or refused to acknowledge it, and it could be disruptive to them. "The Myth of Er" in Book X of Plato's Republic tells of the dead arriving at a barren wasteland called the "Plain of Lethe" through which the river Ameles ("careless") runs. The initiated, or those who had achieved a high degree of spiritual transformation through the mysteries, were taught to seek the river of memory called "Mnemosyne". However, due to the conditions of the age in which we today, and this included Joan's age although Steiner reveals that the conditions of that time were quite

The challenge and task of a genuine service on behalf of the Spiritual Hierarchies is fundamentally based on the willingness to give up one's life, name, and ego for the welfare, future, and freedom of others. One must be willing to hurl one's self into the dragon's breath, as it were. This prospect is easy to contemplate and, perhaps, possible to ponder in an academic context. The reality of it only becomes clear, and tangible, when one gets into the field, as it were. Joan recognized the validity of her spiritual guides whose form and substance manifested through genuine clairvoyance and clairaudient faculties which others did not possess. Therefore, she could not turn to a friend, confidant, or informed source to get a valid opinion on her visions. They were hers and hers alone. As a result, Joan accepted the validity of her spiritual visions and followed the counsel of her guardians to the very end including the decision to reject every path forward that would have saved her own life and interrupted the culmination of her divine mission.

So, regardless of how traumatic Joan's death was, and it was brutally traumatic, Joan perceived that she was compelled to pass into the eternal realm of the spiritual worlds having fulfilled her mission. She would stand before the Christ, the Archangel Michael, the Saints, and the leaders of humanity with a clear conscience prepared to move forward to the next task...whatever that was. As a human being with a special task, even with foreknowledge and inner insights, one still has to physically pass through the painful experience of birth, life, and the path of martyrdom. Even with direct knowledge, this path requires profound and sincere faith and courage.

Genuine martyrs throughout human history, including those who served a broader purpose for others but were not serving the same spiritual tasks as Joan, have been compelled to accept their fate under tragic circumstances. This surrendering to one's fate is a difficult test. It requires forgoing one's egotism, pride, selfishness, form, and corporeal future for an idea and purpose that extends beyond one's immediate wants, needs, or desires. Like Joan, that purpose extends beyond the horizon of physical sight. It rises above time and carries over into the eternal. Countless soldiers

---

different from today, a certain degree of amnesia is a necessary part of the reincarnating process. Each person passes through a necessary path, according to their karma, of unfolding their consciousness throughout their lifetime and reforming a bridge and perception of the spiritual worlds.

throughout history have fought for genuine freedom, regardless of the time period, and have given their lives in authentic self-effacing acts of sacrifice for a purpose that, perhaps, they viewed as being just and true. Genuine sacrifices are made during wars that are otherwise selfless acts that are done for the right reasons. These martyrdoms always change the future and are never wasted. Steiner reveals that the "giving back" of one's deeds to the universe is a tangible and ongoing aspect of human transformation and carries forward from one life to the next.

So, after Joan's martyrdom in 1431 when the course was set right, a new impulse emerged gradually over time within the consciousness of humanity and every human being has changed because of it. Outside of the liberation of France, this new spiritual impulse was not something that one could point to in physical terms. Rather, it is an aspect of the human being that perceived things in a new way. The new impulse affected England, France, and all of Europe who, in turn, influenced the world over the coming centuries. This new impulse cultivated the impulse that gave rise to the United States, Central and South America, Australia, South Africa, and the cultural impulses that now flow into the East through globalization. It has directly led to the current world environment. In reality, and in spiritual-cultural terms, England, Europe, and the world have as much to be grateful for as France does to Joan's mission and contribution.

The quest of the Grail, and the one who seeks transformation, is a unique process of "building-up" and "giving-back" to the world and the universe. This genuine task, which frequently expresses itself in martyrdom at its transition point, characterizes all of those who lead difficult spiritual missions on behalf of the directives of the divine spiritual beings who oversee humanity's progress. This "giving-back", as it were, completes the mission for every human soul who has walked the path of spiritual martyrdom throughout human history and carries the spirit of the Christ within them. Thus, Joan's mission could not have been properly completed without her martyrdom. It was a necessary, and integrated, aspect of serving a mission in the way that she did. This applied principle finds its apex and ultimate expression in the martyrdom of the Christ at Golgotha in 33AD when the entire world was imbued, and forever changed, with His transformative impulse. It inspires and compels all of those who came, and are destined to come, after Him... The Forces that He released into the world, and gradually unfold through the world over time, came into being through the crucifixion.

Accepting the reality of her physical death, Our Maid walked down the path of her destiny with an open heart and in the full knowledge that it was going to be a painful transition, yet it was necessary to accomplish her mission on behalf of Christ-Jesus and the Archangel Michael who actively work on behalf of the world. Joan died in agony and pain. However, also within her was the direct knowledge that she would, as promised by the spiritual guides who communicated directly to her, transition to the other side of the grave in paradise and the spiritual worlds. The pain would come to an end. Her mission would be accomplished. Her life would continue.

> "Joan of Arc on going through the gate of death was prepared to continue contributing to the work of shaping events after her death, to share in the work whatever her form of existence. And she did so. What the spiritual powers have to bring about will be brought about whatever the external conditions may be. Joan's adversaries were able to bring about her death, to mount the strongest possible attack against her, as it were. They were not able to prevent her mission."[202]

It is the author's contention, and belief, that Joan's destiny was not to simply retire into anonymity and rest, as it were, in the spiritual worlds as is widely envisaged by a materialistic humanity. Rather, this special and unique individual, who lived and died as a genuine martyr, has carried her special mission forward into new areas and tasks where she continues to work on behalf of the Christ, the Archangel Michael, and the spiritual leaders of humanity who oversee and guide the welfare and transformation of humanity for all time...

Thus, in light of Joan's mission from a spiritual perspective, it becomes clear why she did not opt to take advantage of several alternatives that were offered to her during her trial. It would not have been enough for Joan to simply lead the French armies to victory, negotiate a way out after she had been captured, and then retire to another country or her home village and live out a peaceful life. This was not possible anyways and the English had no intention of honoring any agreement they offered Joan. Surely, Joan, as a human being, wanted to preserve her life. She was, after

---

[202] Steiner, Rudolf. The Destinies of Individuals and Nations, The Nature of the Christ Impulse and the Michaelic Sprit Serving It, Lecture 5. Berlin, January 19, 1915.

all, not eager to die a painful death. However, Joan exhibited fearless determination in the face of threats and adversity knowing the consequences of recanting on the promises that she made to her spiritual guardians, who in fact guard all of humanity, as is revealed in her trial records.

So, in light of Our Maid, Joan of Arc, let it be known that some walk amongst us that have forsaken their vanity and egotism. Some have given up their self-interest and, if need be, their lives purely on behalf of others and a larger task. Joan was one of those rare people who remained loyal to her spiritual guides, the Christ, her family, and her principles. instead of pursuing her egotism, she chose the path of service.

In light of all the honors bestowed upon Joan over the centuries in terms of sainthood, royal affirmation of her family's name, and the recognition that she has received posthumously at the national level, I think Joan would simply have shrugged those accolades off and acknowledged how just ridiculous vainly labels are. Victory is what Joan was after. And that is what she achieved. She would never succumb to notions of vanity, egotism, and self-glorification. So, in the wisdom of hindsight, I suspect that Joan, in the Spirit of the Christ and a victory over the Luciferic powers, would have pushed all of those vainly things away. In fact, they might have irritated her.

Joan carried, and still carries as someone who is deeply connected to the ongoing transformative impulse of humanity on behalf of the Christ, a great heart and spirit within her that should, and will, be remembered for all time...

Appendix A: Chronology

The following timeline provides a summary overview of key historical events in the Hundred Years' War with an emphasis on Joan's life. There are several ways to view this timeline, however, this summary shall consider historical events. It is not intended to provide an exhaustive view. As the timeline moves into the years 1428-1431, it becomes more detailed. The specific days, and in some cases perhaps even months, should be considered as approximations as researchers and historians frequently do not agree on precise dates. Significant victories for the French peoples, and important turning points, as perceived by the author are marked by a Cross of Lorraine symbol (‡).

1328   The death of the French King Charles IV la Bel ("the Fair") without direct heir/issue. His father, Philip the Fair, was responsible for the suppression and execution of the Knights Templars on Friday, October 13, 1307. Philip, Count of Valois, cousin to Charles the Fair, becomes King Philip VI of France.

1340   King Edward III of England, nephew of Charles the Fair, assumes the title King of France and asserts his authority over the French peoples whom he views as being his subjects. Thus, the Hundred Years' War begins in terms of political and military policy.

1346   The French forces were decisively defeated at the Battle of Crécy. The French army was commanded by King Philip VI and the English by Edward the Black Prince; the son of Edward III. An estimated 40,000 men participate. The French attacked the English while they were traversing northern France resulting in an English victory and heavy loss of life among the French. It is a decisive turning point for the English.

1346-   The Black Death, or the Bubonic Plague, swept through France
1353   and England. An estimated 50% of the French population dies and a comparable percentage of English perish as well. The French, however, appear to suffer more losses than the English in human and economic terms. This led to a serious economic crisis in France and England but England recovered more quickly. While precise numbers are not known, a large percentage of the population dies across Europe and North Africa as well.

1350   A French attack on the English-occupied port city of Calais resulted in a rout and victory for Edward III at what is known today as the <u>Battle of Calais.</u> Some 2-4,000 soldiers participated. A bribe-truce had been negotiated between the French commander Geoffrey de Charny and Amerigo of Pavia who was an Italian officer of the city garrison, to open a gate for the French. King Edward III became aware of the plot and personally led his household knights and the Calais garrison in a surprise counter-attack. The French were routed by Edward's smaller force with significant losses and all of the French leaders were captured or killed.

       *This year also marks the death of the French King Philip VI and the accession of his son King John II "the Good".

1356   The French were heavily defeated at the <u>Battle of Poitiers</u>. Edward the Black Prince and son of Edward III led an army of English, Welsh, Breton, and Gascon troops many of whom were veterans of the Battle of Crécy. They were attacked by a larger French force led by King John II that also included allied Scottish forces who had, in turn, won their independence from England in 1314 in the final battle of the Scottish War of Independence that is remembered for the efforts of men such as William Wallace and Robert the Bruce. The Scottish would come to play a supporting role in the French quest for independence and would provide forces who fought under various French leaders, including Joan of Arc, over the course of the Hundred Years' War.

       The result of this pivotal French defeat was that King John II, his son, and a large portion of the French nobility were captured, ransomed, or imprisoned.

1360   Most of the lands of Western France are ceded to King Edward III in a truce to cease hostilities with the <u>Treaty of Brétigny</u> later ratified as the <u>Treaty of Calais.</u>

1364   The death of the French King John II and the accession of King Charles V "the Wise".

1377   Death of King Edward III and ascension of his grandson King Richard II, also known as Richard of Bordeaux, reigns until he was deposed/usurped in 1399 by the future King Henry IV. This event eventually leads to a dispute in England and the Wars of the

Roses in the wake of Joan's death in 1431. Richard's father was Edward the Black Prince of Wales, and heir apparent to Edward III, who died in 1376 of illness.

1380   The death of Charles the Wise and the coronation of Charles VI occurs at the age of twelve. This leads to a dispute between Louis, Duke of Anjou, and Philip the Bold, Duke of Burgundy who were both guardians of Charles VI regarding who would oversee the affairs of the French state.

1384   King Charles VI weds Isabeau of Bavaria.

1388   King Charles VI assumes political control over France.

1389   Isabeau of Bavaria makes her royal entry into Paris. At that time, Paris was considered the political capital of France.

1392   King Charles VI begins to suffer from unexplained bouts of mental illness and experiences intermittent spells of madness and incapacitation for the rest of his life. Rivalry for control over France once again breaks out between Philip of Burgundy and Louis of Orléans.

1396   King Richard II of England marries Isabelle, daughter of Charles VI, and drops the title King of France thus signaling his desire to pull back from English control of French-held territories.

1397   Richard II returns the city of Brest to French control.

1399-   Richard II is formally deposed by Henry IV of Lancaster in 1399
1400   and died in the Tower of London in 1400-1401.

1403   The birth of the Dauphin Charles, whom with the help of Joan was to be later crowned King Charles VII of France.

1404   The death of Philip the Bold, Duke of Burgundy. He is succeeded by John "the Fearless". Queen Isabeau, wife of Charles VI, now openly consorts with her brother-in-law, Louis of Orléans. This leads to rumors that the Dauphin, Charles VII, is the product of this relationship. As a result, the rivalry for power intensifies between the Dukes of Burgundy and Orléans.

1407   Louis of Orléans is murdered by agents of John the Fearless. John publicly accepts responsibility The murder of Louis sparked a blood feud and the intensification of a civil war between the Burgundians and the French royal family that divided France for the next 28 years ending only with the <u>Treaty of Arras</u> in 1435.

1408   Most of the Doctors at the University of Paris, including Pierre Cauchon, read a justification of the murder of Louis, thus signaling publicly the University's and Bishop Cauchon's loyalties to the English. This is no doubt due to bribes and promises of safety by the English who longed to hold Paris as the center of French political and economic activity. Bishop Cauchon's pro-English sympathies would factor heavily in future events as he would become the leading instigator and prosecutor of Joan of Arc.

1409   A truce is established between John the Fearless and Charles the son of Louis of Orléans.

1410   Charles of Orléans marries the daughter of Bernard VII of Armagnac, who becomes the leader of the Orléans faction known afterward as the "Armagnacs".

1411   Charles of Orléans, supported by Bernard VII of Armagnac, challenges John the Fearless, who is now supported by Queen Isabeau who has switched allegiances.

1412   January 6. The birth of Jeanne at Domrémy. This small town is located in a contested section of France that was regularly targeted by Burgundian and English raiding parties.

1413   Henry V of Lancaster, son of Henry IV, becomes King of England. Henry V asserts his authority over France and the final act of the Hundred Years' War begins with his aggressive military strategy.

1415   October 25. The French suffer a severe defeat at the muddy Battle of Agincourt under the leadership of Henry V. The English forces were outnumbered more than 2 to 1 (approximately 25,000 soldiers participated) and achieved a tremendous victory in the face of overwhelming odds due to the use of the longbow (where the French relied on heavily armored cavalry). Charles, Duke of Orléans was taken prisoner and was a serious setback for the Armagnacs. He is imprisoned in England and later freed in 1440 as predicted by Joan of Arc before her death in 1431.

1416   John the Fearless, leader of Burgundy, signs a pact between the Burgundians and the English thus dividing France into separate spheres of political and economic autonomy. France is essentially divided into three separate political entities.

1417   The English renew the offensive in Normandy. The Burgundians attack Paris that was held by Bernard of Armagnac and the Dauphin Charles. John the Fearless kidnaps Queen Isabeau and sets her up with a sham government at Troyes.

1418   May 29: John the Fearless of Burgundy captures Paris. King Charles VI was taken prisoner. The Burgundians assume control of Paris.

1418-   Henry V leads the extended Siege of Rouen which is a stronghold
19   of French political and economic power and inhabited by some 20,000 citizens. Rouen falls in 1419.

        John the Fearless of Burgundy is assassinated at Montereau by followers of the Dauphin. Sympathy swings to the Burgundians.

        Philip the Good, ascended Duke of Burgundy, signs a pact in the name of the captive king Charles VI with Henry V of England. The agreement is that Henry V shall marry Catherine of France, Daughter of Charles VI and Queen Isabeau. This is significant because the Queen allows for the open implication that the Dauphin, Charles VII, is illegitimate.

1420   May 21: Treaty of Troyes. The Dauphin Charles VII is eliminated from succession to the crown of France which now passes directly to Henry V after the future death of Charles VI that occurs in 1422. Henry V marries Catherine of France. Pierre Cauchon is made "Bishop of Beauvais" for his service in the negotiations at the Treaty of Troyes. The Dauphin Charles is officially banished, repudiated by his parents, and prevented from being crowned King of France. He retreats beyond the River Loire to the areas that remain loyal to the French including Berry, Touraine, Poitou, and Midi. He eventually makes his court in Chinon. He marries Marie of Anjou.

1422   King Henry V dies suddenly of illness. King Charles VI also dies. Henry VI of England, now heir to the throne of England and France, is ten months old. The brother of Henry V, John of Lancaster, Duke of Bedford becomes regent of England and English-held lands in France, and with the help of the 13th Duke of Warwick oversees the education and minority of young Henry VI. The Dauphin Charles VII assumes the contested title of King of France.

1423   An agreement is concluded between John, Duke of Bedford, Philip of Burgundy, and John V, Duke of Brittany. The Duke of Bedford marries Anne, the sister of Philip of Burgundy. The Duke of Bedford asserts his authority and control over English interests in France and is, for all intensive purposes, the de facto King of England with Henry VI in his youth and minority at that time.

1424   The English conquest of Normandy is completed.

1424-   Based on Joan's testimony at her trial in Rouen in 1431, she
1426   hears the voices of her spiritual guides for the first time in her father's garden at 13-14 years of age. The annunciation, as it were, of her future role as an inspiration and military leader in France begins to unfold at this time as her spiritual guides establish a conscious bridge of dialogue with Joan which she keeps a closely guarded secret. It can be reasonably inferred that Joan's spiritual guides are preparing her for her mission.

1428   **Jeanne's Mission Begins**
Spring-Summer   The preparations for the English Siege of Orléans begin. Orléans is the gateway to the Loire region and the headquarters area of the Dauphin at Chinon. Beyond this area, there is no retreat. If Orléans falls, so does the Dauphin and so goes France. France stands on the precipice of total defeat to the English and the Burgundians.
April-Midsummer   Joan is notified by her guides to undertake a mission to embark on her mission to save France and that she should go to the bastion/castle of French Captain Robert de Baudricourt at Vaucouleurs. Joan requests official permission to go to the Dauphin in Chinon and make a plea to lead the French as the Maid of Orléans and the fulfillment of an ancient prophecy. It is a dangerous journey to Vaucouleurs and her uncle agrees to be her guardian and chaperon. It would be several months and not until February of 1429, and only

after three attempts by Joan before Captain Baudricourt would allow Joan to go to Chinon.

July

The Siege of Vaucouleurs by the Burgundians and the exodus of inhabitants of Domrémy to a stronghold/castle of Neufchateau.

August

Charles the Dauphin makes a four-month truce with the duke of Burgundy and he agrees to surrender certain Burgundian towns that had recently surrendered to him.

October 12

The Siege of Orléans officially begins.

1429
February 12:

A Heroine Enters the Field

The Battle of the Herrings, also called the Battle of Rouvray, occurs near the town of Rouvray in France just north of Orléans. The battle was the result of an attempt by French and Scottish forces, led by Charles of Bourbon and Sir John Stewart of Darnley, to intercept an English supply convoy headed for the English army at Orléans. The English had been laying siege to the city since the previous October. This supply convoy was escorted by an English force under Sir John Fastolf and had been outfitted in Paris, from whence it had departed sometime earlier. The battle was decisively won by the English.

February 23

Probable date of Joan's departure from Vaucouleurs for the Dauphin's court at Chinon.

March 6

Probable date of Joan's arrival at Chinon. She has to wait to see the Dauphin as she is screened and questioned by his advisors. She awaits a meeting with Charles at a nearby hotel/lodging house.

March 9

Joan is granted permission to see the Dauphin and has her first interview.

March 9-22.	At the Dauphin's insistence, Joan proceeded to Poitiers to be examined by the church Doctors and authorities there who were loyal to the French (as opposed to those in Paris who were aligned with the English and Burgundians). With the clerical verdict that she posed no threat, Charles commissions her to lead the army to Orléans.
March 22	Charles provided Joan with a suit of plate armor, a banner, a formal page, and heralds. The army is recruited, organized, and prepared to move on Orléans with Joan as the lead.
	Joan issues her first public letter of challenge to the English to leave Orléans and France.
April 28	The French royal army under Joan's leadership leaves the town of Blois for Orléans.
April 29	Joan and the French army arrive at Orléans and enter the main city before the English can prevent her from doing so. The French army brings much-needed supplies, food, and support. The Battle of Orléans officially begins and lasts only 9 days.
May 4	A tactical victory for the French is achieved with the capture of the "Bastille of Saint-Loup" at Orléans. The English fall back to the "Bastille of the Augustins."
May 6	The French captured the Bastille of the Augustins. The French are now in firm command and begin an assault of the "Bastille of the Tourelles" that is the main road for entrance into the fortified town of Orléans.
May 7	The French capture the Bastille of the Tourelles. Joan is wounded by an arrow and she is temporarily pulled out of action. She recovers and reenters the battle and rallies the army to victory.

May 8.‡	Victory. The Siege of Orléans is lifted and the English are routed. The English retreat from the area and this victory mark the key turning point in the Hundred Years' War.
	Joan notifies King Charles VII that "I will only be with you for one year. It is needful, then that you use me to the full."
May 9	Joan and Jean d'Orléans, Count of Dunois (the official royal Duke in charge of the city) leave Orléans for Loches to meet with the Dauphin.

Despite the continued vacillation of King Charles VII and his desire to pull back and acquiesce to English and Burgundian demands and threats, Joan influences him to continue the military strategy. As a result, a string of significant victories followed the liberation of Orléans and the tide of the war turned to the French.[203] Charles, however, vacillates unequivocally. This indecisiveness, or rather decision not to act, reaches an apex with the failure of the Siege of Paris led by Joan when he decides to lift the siege after only two weeks and retreat.

June 12‡	The city of Jargeau is captured by the French.
June 15‡	The city of Meung-Sur-Loire is captured by the French.
June 17‡	The city of Beaugency is captured by the French.
June 18‡	The French achieve a major victory at the Battle of Patay, which is just north of Orléans. The English garrisons withdraw to Paris.
June 29	French army leaves the city of Gien and moves toward Reims.
July 3‡	The French army left Gien on June 29 on the march toward Reims and accepted the conditional surrender of Auxerre that was held by the Burgundians.

---

[203] Orléans is an ancient city that has existed since at least the 4th century AD. It has been everything from a simple trading post to a rival with Paris for the center of royal government. After the year 1344, all of the dukes of Orléans were close relatives of the French Kings. Therefore, Orléans was one of the most important cities in France from a spiritual and political perspective.

July 10‡	The <u>Victory at Troyes</u> after a bloodless siege. The Anglo-Burgundian forces retreat.
July 14‡	Entry of royal army into Chalons.
July 16‡	Charles VII and Joan enter Reims for his coronation.
July 17‡	The coronation of Charles VII takes place with Joan present in the cathedral at Reims.
July 20	Charles VII leaves Reims after his coronation. The royal court negotiated a truce with Duke Philip of Burgundy not to attack Paris.
August 15	The Duke of Bedford led an English force to confront Charles VII's army at the <u>Battle of Montépilloy</u> on August 15 that resulted in a standoff.
September 8	Joan leads an attack on Paris. The city is heavily fortified and under English influence. Despite a wound to the leg from an arrow, Joan remained in the inner trench of Paris until she was carried back to safety by one of the French commanders.
September 21	Charles VII's army under Joan's leadership is disbanded after the failure to take Paris after a period of only two weeks. This siege was ambitious but could have been accomplished with patience and diligence. Sieges of this magnitude required months to achieve. The Siege of Rouen, for example, by King Henry V took 6 months to accomplish.
November 4‡	The <u>Siege of Saint-Pierre-le-Moûtier</u> was victorious for the French.
November 4 to December 24	Joan's <u>Siege of La Charité</u> is unsuccessful after a month. The French withdraw.
December 24	An official patent of nobility is granted to Joan and her family by Charles VII. Her family and the village of Domrémy are granted a tax exemption.

1430

Jan-April/May	A truce was negotiated by Charles VI with the English. Charles, as ever, makes a poor tactical decision. As it turns out, this was a ploy for a time so the English could reinforce their numbers. The winter months result in little activity for Joan who spends at least part of the time in a royal castle at Sully eagerly awaiting operations to begin again. She is carefully monitored by the King's advisors who have grown

	jealous of her prominent role and influence on the king.
January 8	The marriage of Philip the Good of Burgundy to Isabella of Portugal occurs, thus aligning Burgundy and England with a new ally.
April 4	Philip the Good of Burgundy enters the city of Péronne.
April 23	Fresh English reinforcements disembark at the English-held port of Calais and move inland in support of renewed operations against France.
April	Joan leaves the royal castle at Sully to resume operations. She passes through the towns of Melun, Lagny, and Senlis.
May 14	Joan arrives at the besieged fortified city of Compiègne. She departs shortly thereafter as the Burgundians have temporarily withdrawn.
May 18	Joan departs Compiègne and arrives at Soissons.
May 22	A reinforced Burgundian army arrives at Compiègne and a siege begins.
May 23	Joan arrives at Compiègne. She was apprehended after she twice repelled the Burgundian forces. However, she was eventually outflanked by English reinforcements. This was a trap orchestrated by Charles's advisors. As the French forces retreated behind the city walls and the gate was closing, Joan heroically held the line protecting her rearguard as the Burgundians crossed the Oise River and were ambushed. Joan surrendered and her brother Pierre and Jean d'Aulon was taken to Beaurevoir Castle where she was questioned by the Duke of Burgundy.

*The marks a prophetic fulfillment of Joan's that she stated to Charles VII after the victory at Orléans that "I will only be with you for one year. It is needful, then that you use me to the full." |
| June | The University of Paris demands Joan be tried for heresy but they are denied by the Duke of Burgundy who keeps Joan in his possession and offers to sell her to the English. |

July	The journey of Joan of Arc's prosecutor, Bishop Pierre Cauchon, to the Duke of Burgundy occurs where he negotiates to have Joan turned over to the English. Her sale is agreed upon for the final price of 10,000 livres tournois.
October 25	The English lift the prolonged Siege of Compiègne and retreat. This outcome was prophesized by Joan after her capture at Compiègne.
December 23	After being moved between several locations, Joan is finally taken to Rouen for trial under English escort after being sold by the Duke of Burgundy.
1431	The French (Armagnacs) forces loyal to Joan attempted to rescue her several times by launching military campaigns against the fortified city of Rouen during Joan's imprisonment. One assault occurred during the winter of 1430/31, the second in March 1431, and the third in late May 1431. All of these attempts failed.
January 9	The opening of Joan's trial. 17 sessions of questioning would follow during Joan's incarceration over the course of the next 5 months. The first 6 sessions are held in public, the remaining sessions are held in private in Joan's cell.
February 21	First official session of public questioning and interrogation of Joan.
March 10	Private interrogations of Joan begin. These interrogations are held in Joan's prison cell.
March 17	Closing of the "inquiry" period of the trial.
March 27	The indictment against Joan is completed.
April 5	Consultations with ecclesiastical authorities begin.
April 18	The charitable "admonition", or plea, is made to Joan.
May 9	Joan is threatened with torture.
May 19	Response of the University of Paris to the articles of accusation.
May 23	Final admonitions were made to Joan. The official trial concludes.

May 24	The "Abjuration" event takes place at the Saint-Ouen cemetery.[204] Faced with immediate execution on May 24, Joan agreed to renounce wearing men's clothing and sign a document that she would wear women's clothes but only if she was allowed to be given mass and a change in guard from English soldiers to women.
May 27	Joan is not given mass and claims a rape attempt occurred which, based on historical accounts, was blocked by the Duke of Warwick whose living quarters were within an earshot of Joan's cell. Joan realizes that she has been betrayed by the French and that, in actuality, the freedom of France is directly tied to her martyrdom. She reassumes male clothing realizing it means her death.
May 28	The "Relapse" and Final Adjudication of Joan is declared by the court.
May 30‡	Joan is released by the ecclesiastical authorities and officially turned over to the English secular authorities. This is back and forth is political maneuvering. Joan is burned at the stake in the Old Market Place in Rouen in the morning.
June 8	Notification of Joan's execution is sent to the princes of Christendom, many of whom denounced the deed.
December 16	The coronation of Henry VI of England as king of France, in Paris.
1435	Death of John of Lancaster, Duke of Bedford brother of Henry V, and senior leader of the English cause in France.
	Later that year the <u>Treaty of Arras</u> is concluded between France and Burgundy setting in motion events that will lead to England's expulsion from France.
1437	Entry of King Charles VII into Paris and the city shifts from English influence to French. This is a key

---

[204] Joan was taken to a scaffold set up in the cemetery next to Saint-Ouen Church in Rouen and told that she would be burned immediately unless she signed a document renouncing her visions and agreeing to stop wearing soldiers' clothing.

transition in the balance of power in the region to French favor. This is also a fulfillment of Joan's prophecy that the English would be driven out of France within seven years of her death.

1450	King Charles VII orders an inquiry into Joan's trial.
1452	An ecclesiastical inquiry, but not the official trial, into Joan's life begins with Cardinal Guillaume d'Estouteville and Inquisitor Jean Brehal.
1455	After the conclusion of the inquiry, Pope Calixtus II permits Joan's mother and brothers to have an official retrial known as the "Trial of Rehabilitation".
1456	Joan is acquitted and the initial verdict is annulled by the Archbishop of Reims.
1920, May 16.	Joan is canonized by Pope Benedict XV.

Appendix B: Certain Personalities (1400-1431)

The following list is a brief list of individuals, in historical terms, who were connected to Joan and found themselves, per their karmic histories, involved in that chaotic time in human history. Like most everyone, surely these were influenced by her life and death from 1400-1431 in many ways. This is a short and partial list to be sure, but it provides a view into certain individuals who played a role in shaping the landscape of England and France during that period of strife and transformation.

The French

King Charles VII: (1422-1461). Also known as the "Victorious" and "Well-Beloved". Although Charles VII's legacy is certainly overshadowed by the deeds and martyrdom of Joan of Arc and his early reign was marked by indecisiveness, vacillation, and inaction, he was crowned as the anointed king of France and Joan remained faithful to Charles to the last. Through Joan, Charles succeeded in what four generations of his predecessors had failed to accomplish and push the English out of France. He established the University of Poitiers in 1432, and his policies brought some economic prosperity to his subjects. Through Joan, Charles led the French peoples forward and through his prodding, the Trial of Nullification of Joan came to a successful resolution in 1456.

Left: Charles VII by Jean Fouquet, 1444, Louvre, Paris.

The Journey to Chinon

Robert de Baudricourt (1400-1454)**:** In 1429, Robert De Baudricourt's title was captain of the royal garrison at Vaucouleurs. The gateway to Chinon, Robert rejected Joan twice and refused to grant her passage. Unbeknownst to history, she convinced him on her third try. She did not leave, however, before he purchased a knight's armor, a warhorse, supplies, and supplied her with an armed escort. This unexpected turn of events suggests that he, like Charles VII, experienced something of a miracle that convinced him that she was a genuine messenger, or at the very least a seer, from God so he financially endorsed and supported Joan on her mission.

Some suggest that Joan publicly denounced Robert publicly upon her final return to Vaucouleurs and he relented out of fear or pressure, but I find this unlikely. It is more likely that as rumors of the "Maid", who performed little miracles, circulated and people began to journey to Vaucouleurs. Robert could see with his own eyes that a genuine movement and opportunity was beginning. However, Joan had earned something of a reputation as a healer and seer by that time. Her path to convincing others on the French side, as she did with Charles VII, was a peaceful one that utilized her genuine powers of clairvoyance. While no direct evidence exists, my intuition suggests that Joan provided Robert some private miracle, or vision, if you will that convinced him of her unique and special abilities.

Jean de Metz: (1398 – at Least 1456). Accompanied Joan to Chinon. Served as one of the lead knights under Robert de Baudricourt and followed Joan during the campaigns acting as a bodyguard and knight. Later, he testified at her retrial in 1456. His death date is unknown.

> "I and Bertrand de Poulengy, with two of my men, Colet de Vienne, the King's Messenger, and the Archer Richard, conducted the Maid to the King, who was then at Chinon. The journey was made at the expense of Bertrand de Poulengy and myself. We travelled for the most part at night, for fear of the Burgundians and the English, who were masters of the roads. We journeyed eleven days, always riding towards the said town of Chinon. On the way, I asked her many times if she would really do all she said. "Have no fear," she answered us, "what I am commanded to do, I will do; my brothers in Paradise have told me how to act: it is four or five years since my

brothers in Paradise and my Lord---that is, God---told me that I must go and fight in order to regain the kingdom of France.

"On the way, Bertrand and I slept every night by her---Joan being at my side, fully dressed. She inspired me with such respect that for nothing in the world would I have dared to molest her; also, never did I feel towards her---I say it on oath---any carnal desire. On the way she always wished to hear Mass. She said to us: "If we can, we shall do well to hear Mass." But, for fear of being recognized, we were only able to hear it twice. I had absolute faith in her. Her words and her ardent faith in God inflamed me. I believe she was sent from God; she never swore, she loved to attend Mass, she confessed often, and was zealous in giving alms. Many times, was I obliged to hand out to her the money she gave for the love of God. While we were with her, we found her always good, simple, pious, an excellent Christian, well-behaved, and God-fearing. When we arrived at Chinon, we presented ourselves to the King's Court and Council. I know she had there to submit to long enquiries."[205]

Bertrand de Poulengy (1392-at Least 1456): Very little is known about his life. He is believed to have been born sometime around 1392 in Champagne. He accompanied Joan to Chinon and served as a leading knight under Robert de Baudricourt. He surely followed Joan during the campaign. He later testified at Joan's retrial in 1456. Bertrand's death date is unknown.

Richard the Archer: Not much is known of this young man who accompanied Jean and Bertrand to Chinon as Joan's bodyguards and escorts. As Robert adopted Joan's mission into his heart and invested her so heavily, this man surely was one of Robert de Baudricourt's most skilled archers. He followed Joan and fought with her during the campaigns, only later to disappear from history. Nothing is known of his birth or death years. Some have suggested that he was the servant of Colet de Vienne, the messenger of Charles VII.

Colet de Vienne: A messenger of Charles VII who acted as a runner between Joan, Charles, and other captains. He appears to have escorted

---

[205] Testimony of Jean de Metz at Joan's retrial between 1452-1456 who was assigned to protect her by Robert de Baudricourt on her way to Chinon. Jean, and Raymond, accompanied Joan through the campaign against the English and fought by Joan's side.

Joan to Chinon with Jean, Richard the Archer, Bertrand, and two additional guards. For him to be involved in this way indicates that Charles must have been notified in advance that Joan was coming to Chinon and he thereby sent a messenger to escort her back. Presumably, he carried messages between Joan and Charles VII and also acted as a soldier and direct line of communication between the two while she was on campaign. Nothing else is known of him historically.

Two Guards to Chinon: Two additional guards accompanied Joan to Chinon. Their names are known as Julien (servant to Bertrand) and Jean of Honnecourt (servant of Jean de Metz). Presumably, they fought with Joan on her campaigns but no historical evidence survives that corroborates that theory.

Campaign
Étienne de Vignolles, "La Hire": (1390-1443). Known for his poor language and rough disposition, La Hire was one of those who were converted by Joan and reformed his wayward ways and renounced profanity, and attended mass diligently at Joan's prodding and chastising. The nickname "La Hire" could be from the French "hedgehog" ("hérisson"). La Hire joined Charles VII in 1418. Although not a noble, La Hire was regarded as a very capable military leader as well as an accomplished rider. He was a close comrade of Joan of Arc. He was one of the few military leaders who believed in her and the inspiration she brought, and he fought alongside her at Orléans. At the Battle of Patay, La Hire commanded the vanguard (center body of the army). La Hire was known for praying before going into battle due to Joan's influence. In 1430, La Hire captured the English held fortification of Château Gaillard. He was imprisoned in Dourdan in the spring of 1431. He won the Battle of Gerberoy in 1435 and was made Captain of Normandy in 1438. His last two major military engagements occurred in 1440 at Pontoise where he assisted Dunois to capture it from the English, and in 1442 he assisted Charles of Orleans in capturing La Réole.

John II (Duc) of Alençon (1409 –1476) was a French nobleman. He succeeded his father as Duke of Alençon and Count of Perche as a minor in 1415, after the latter's death at the Battle of Agincourt. He is best known as a general in the Last Phase of the Hundred Years' War and for his role as a comrade-in-arms of Joan of Arc. He was held prisoner until 1429 at Le Crotoy, paying 200,000 Saluts d'Or for his ransom. He sold all he possessed to the English and his fief of Fougères to the Duke of Brittany. After Alençon's capture, the Duke of Bedford, regent of King Henry VI, took control of his duchy. He would not regain Alençon until 1449 but remained the titular duke in the eyes of the French crown. When he left prison, Jean d'Alençon was known as "the poorest man in France".

Jean d'Aulon (1390–1458): served as one of Joan's bodyguards and a squire. He took part in the rout of the English at the Siege of Montargis in 1427 where a French relief force of about 1,600 men under Jean de Dunois, the Bastard of Orléans, was able to drive off a superior English force of about 3,000 men led by the Earl of Warwick (all military captains fell under the command of John of Lancaster, Duke of Bedford). Along with a small force of about 500 men, Jean was with Joan during her capture at the Burgundian siege of Compiègne when she was caught outside the city walls. The bridge was retracted before she could make her way behind the city walls. Later, he became Chamberlain to the king and Captain-Governor of the castle at Pierre-Scize.

John Dunois, the Bastard of Orléans: Jean d'Orléans, Count of Dunois (1402–1468), known as the "Bastard of Orléans" (French: bâtard d'Orléans) or simply Jean de Dunois, was a French military leader during who participated in military campaigns with Joan of Arc. His nickname, the "Bastard of Orléans", was a term of higher hierarchy and respect, since it acknowledged him as a first cousin to the king and acting head of a cadet branch of the royal family during his half-brother's captivity. In 1439 he received the county of Dunois from his half-brother Charles, Duke of Orléans, and later king Charles VII made him count of Longueville.

Georges de la Trémoille (1382-1446): The Grand Chamberlain of France and the Dauphin's lieutenant general for Burgundy. Trémoïlle was Joan's leading enemy at court and it is widely accepted that he had in luring into the area of Compiègne to be captured by Burgundian forces. It is reputed that Trémoïlle convinced Charles VII not to aid Joan after her capture at Compiègne. Two years after Joan's death, Trémoïolle's continuing unpopularity caused an attempt on his life. In 1439 he was a part of the failed Praguerie, the attempt to overthrow the aristocracy. His banishment from court finally occurred in 1453. Trémoïlle died in 1466.

Jean Poton de Xaintrailles (1380-1461). Jean was one of the chief lieutenants of Joan of Arc. In 1454 he was appointed a Marshal of France.

He fought at the battle of Verneuil in 1424 and was severely wounded beside Joan of Arc at the Siege of Orléans in 1429. He was captured by William de Beauchamp, 9th Earl of Warwick in a skirmish at Savignies near Beauvais in 1431. In 1433 he was exchanged for the English leader John Talbot. Jean Poton fought numerous battles alongside Joan of Arc during the Loire Campaign. He remained a lifelong supporter. With Captain La Hire, he even tried, albeit in vain, to rescue Joan in Rouen after she was captured. Believing Joan was being held captive in Compiègne, Jean Poton captured it, only to learn that Joan had already been moved to Rouen.

The English

King Henry V (1386-1422): also called Henry of Monmouth. Despite his relatively short reign, Henry's military successes in the Hundred Years' War against France made England one of the strongest military powers in Europe, and the impetus for British imperialism that he inspired reached an apex during his reign. He was immortalized in Shakespeare's plays. During the reign of his father Henry IV, Henry gained military experience fighting the Welsh during the revolt of Owain Glyndŵr and against the powerful aristocratic Percy family of Northumberland at the Battle of Shrewsbury. Henry acquired an increasing role in England's government due to the king's declining health, but disagreements between father and son led to political conflict. After his father died in 1413, Henry V assumed control of England and asserted his claim against an ongoing English entitlement to the French throne. This treaty had long been accepted as a passive agreement at that time.

In 1415, Henry embarked on the war with France. His military successes culminated in his famous victory at the Battle of Agincourt (1415) that brought France to her knees and near the brink of ruination. Taking advantage of political divisions within France, he conquered large portions of the kingdom, resulting in Normandy's occupation by the English for the first time since the reign of Edward III. After months of negotiation with Charles VI of France, the Treaty of Troyes (1420) recognized Henry V as regent and heir apparent to the French throne, and he was subsequently married to Charles VI's daughter, Catherine of Valois. He died of illness while on the campaign and the crown fell to his son, Henry VI, who was born in 1421 the year before his death.

King Henry VI (1421-1461): King of England from 1422 to 1461 and again from 1470 to 1471. The only child of Henry V, he succeeded to the English throne at the age of nine months upon his father's death, and succeeded to the French throne on the death of his maternal grandfather, Charles VI, shortly afterward. Henry inherited the war with France while just a baby. He is the only English monarch to have been crowned King of France in 1431.

During his early reign, several people were ruling during his minority, and this time period saw the pinnacle of English power in France but the subsequent military, diplomatic, and economic problems had seriously endangered the English cause by the time Henry was declared fit to rule in 1437. Surrounded by poor advisors, Henry VI inherited a realm that was in a difficult financial and political position and was faced with setbacks in France and divisions among the nobility at home. Unlike his father, Henry was timid, shy, passive, well-intentioned. He was averse to conflict and warfare and was known for his passive disposition. He has also been described as mentally unstable and fell into a comatose state on at least two occasions. His reign saw the gradual loss of the English lands in France. In 1445 Henry married Charles VII's niece, the ambitious and strong-willed Margaret of Anjou. Things continued to deteriorate for England's interest in France and by 1453 the port of Calais was Henry's only remaining territory on the continent.

With Henry vacillating, power was sought and exercised by quarrelsome nobles who persecuted one another. Combatting factions arose and this gave rise to a general state of disorder in the country. Regional magnates and soldiers returning from France formed groups who aligned under different nobles who fought with one another. These competing groups terrorized each other's lands, paralyzed the courts, and wreaked havoc in the government. Queen Margaret did not remain passive and took advantage of the situation to make herself an effective power player behind the throne.

Amidst the many military failures in France and a collapse of law and order in England, the Queen and her followers came under accusations, especially from Henry VI's popular cousin Richard, 3rd Duke of York, of misconduct of the war in France and misrule of the country. Starting in 1453, Henry had at least two mental breakdowns, and tensions mounted between Margaret and Richard of York over control of the government over the question of succession to the English throne. Civil war broke out in 1455 leading to a long period of dynastic conflict now known as the Wars of the Roses. Henry was deposed on March 4, 1461, by Richard's son who took the throne as Edward IV (1442-1483) by way of the Battle of Towton. Despite Margaret continuing to lead a resistance against Edward, Henry was captured by Edward's forces in 1465 and imprisoned in the Tower of London. Henry was restored to the throne during an uprising by Edward's cousin, Richard Neville 16th Duke of Warwick in 1470, but Edward managed to regain power in 1471 after defeating Henry VI's only son and heir, Edward of Westminster, in battle and imprisoning Henry once again.

Henry died in the Tower. Definitive evidence of who Henry's murderer had never been proven and someone may have acted on their own initiative without Edward IV's consent. Whatever the case, Henry VI left a legacy of educational reform by founding Eton College, King's College, Cambridge, and All Souls College, Oxford. Shakespeare wrote a trilogy of plays about his life, depicting him as a passive king who was heavily influenced by Queen Margaret.

John of Lancaster, 1st Duke of Bedford (1389-1435): Brother of Henry V and leading commander in France during the last part of the Hundred Years' War. acted as regent of France for his nephew Henry VI. Despite his military and administrative talent, thanks to the efforts of Joan of Arc the situation in France had severely deteriorated for the English by the time of his death. Bedford was a capable administrator and captain, and his effective management of the war brought the English to the height of their power in France. After Henry V died in 1422, Bedford was the leading English representative in France. By 1434-35, his efforts were thwarted by political divisions at home and the wavering of England's only ally in the Burgundians. In the last years of Bedford's life, the conflict devolved into a war of attrition, and he became increasingly unable to gather the necessary funds to prosecute the conflict. Bedford died during the congress of Arras in 1435, just as Burgundy was preparing to abandon the English cause and conclude a separate peace with Charles VII of France.

Thomas Montagu, 4th Earl of Salisbury (1388-1428): One of the most important leaders of the English during the period leading up to Joan of Arc's mission, Thomas was invested as earl until 1421. He fought at the siege of Harfleur and the Battle of Agincourt. Montagu fought in various other campaigns in France in the following years. In 1419 he held an independent command, and was appointed lieutenant-general of Normandy and created Count of Perche, as part of Henry V's policy of creating Norman titles for his followers. Although he was employed on some diplomatic missions, he played a minor role in the politics of England, he spent most of his life at work in France, leading troops in various skirmishes and sieges. In 1423, he was appointed governor of Champagne, and in 1425, he captured the city of Le Mans. After a year in England, he returned to a position of command in 1428. Thomas was wounded during the siege of Orléans when the tower he was occupying was hit by a cannonball. There are conflicting reports on the nature of his wound; Enguerrand de Monstrelet states a piece of stone from the window 'carried away part of his face.' He died days later at Meung-Sur-Loire on November 3, 1428.

John Talbot, 1st Earl of Shrewsbury (1404-1453): John was a deputy commander of English forces under John Lancaster, Duke of Bedford during the Hundred Years' War. He served in campaigns in Wales (1404-1413) and Ireland (1414-11419) before fighting in France. He fought at Verneuil in 1424 and thus earned the Order of the Garter. He was leading the English forces during the unsuccessful siege of Orléans in 1429, which was Joan's first battle and victory. Talbot was taken by the French at the Battle of Patay in June 1429 and was a severe defeat for the English. After his release in 1433, he continued fighting for the English in the years that followed with several victories. He died in 1453 just before the escalation of the Wars of the Roses under Richard, 3rd Duke of York against Henry VI.

Richard Beauchamp, 13th Earl of Warwick (1389-1439): Beauchamp played a leading role for the English during this period. He was born in 1380 at Salwarpe in Worcestershire. At the age of sixteen, he was given the Order of the Garter. Following his father's death in 1401, he was given a knighthood in the Order of the Bath. Beauchamp led a pilgrimage to Rome and the Holy Land in 1408 and became a member of King Henry V's privy council upon his return. Interestingly, on the return trip, he went through Russia and Eastern Europe and in 1410 he tried to join the order after the battle of Grunwald. Due to his faithful service and close friendship with Henry V, Beauchamp was named as Henry VI's mentor and protector. Both Beauchamp and Henry VI were in France during Joan's trial and Warwick was present during Joan's execution.

He is also remembered as being the one responsible for overseeing Joan's imprisonment during her trial. Joan was lodged in the castle of Bouvreuil when she was taken to Rouen on December 23, 1430. Beauchamp was among those who paid the judges at Rouen, but he also went to great lengths to care for the welfare of Joan as a prisoner defending her from being assaulted on at least two occasions. He died in Rouen on April 30, 1439, and was buried in the castle chapel in Warwick, England.

Sir William Glasdale (died 1429): An English commander during the Siege of Orleans, he commanded the garrison of St. Jean-le-Blanc and he defended the Tourelles with 800 men in May 1429. Joan of Arc demanded that the English return to their island and Glasdale is remembered for insulting Joan in some fashion as a retort. Glasdale was killed in the ensuing battle and is portrayed in some reenactments as a watershed moment during the battle.

Notable Participants at the Trial of 1431
Many individuals took part in the Trial of 1431. Many of these legates, lawyers, scribes, bishops, and aristocrats came and went throughout the trial. Some of the testimony of these people can be found in the transcripts of the Trial of Nullification/Rehabilitation (1452-1456). Some of these people are quoted throughout this work where quotes were used.[206]

Bishop Pierre Cauchon of Beauvais (1371-1442): was Bishop of Beauvais from 1420 to 1432. A strong partisan of English interests in France during the latter years of the Hundred Years' War, his role in arranging the execution of Joan of Arc led most subsequent observers to condemn his extension of secular politics into an ecclesiastical trial. The Catholic Church overturned his verdict in 1456 and he was excommunicated posthumously in 1457. The bishop is a leading figure in the Joan of Arc story after she was captured at Compiègne.

Maître Guillaume d'Estivet: Someone who was a part of Joan's trial in Rouen in 1431 reputed for his poor behavior, ill-temper, and determination to chastise and insult Joan repeatedly. On at least one occasion, he accosted Joan verbally and Joan, obviously having to deal with his insults and short temper on a regular basis, was seen defending herself. It appears from surviving transcripts that Joan never lost her confidence or will to defend herself...

> "In the same way, Maître Guillaume d'Estivet got into the prison, feigning to be a prisoner—as Loyseleur had done. This d'Estivet was

---

[206] The Retrial of 1456. Refer to the English translation of the trial files from 1902. From the book: Jeanne d'Arc Maid of Orléans Deliverer of France. Edited by T. Douglas Murray.

Promoter, and in this matter was much affected towards the English, whom he desired to please. He was a bad man, and often during the Process spoke ill of the notaries and of those who, as he saw, wished to act justly; and he often cruelly insulted Jeanne, calling her foul names. I think that, in the end of his days, he was punished by God; for he died miserably. He was found dead in a drain outside the gates of Rouen."[207]

Jean Tressard, Secretary to the King of England: was seen returning from the execution exclaiming in great agitation, "We are all ruined, for a good and holy person was burned."

Bishop of Therouanne, brother of John of Luxembourg whose troops had captured Joan, was said to have wept bitterly.

Geoffroy Therage, Executioner: confessed to Martin Ladvenu and Isambart de la Pierre afterward, saying that "...he had a great fear of being damned, [that] he had burned a saint."

The Burgundians (Leading Personalities)

Philip III, Duke of Burgundy (1396-1467): was Duke of Burgundy from 1419 until his death. He was a member of a cadet line of the Valois dynasty. During his reign, the Burgundian State reached the apex of its prosperity and became a leading center of the arts. Philip is known in history for his administrative reforms, his patronage of Flemish artists, and the capture of Joan of Arc. In political affairs, he drifted between alliances with the English and the French in an attempt to improve his dynasty's power base. He played an important role in the history of the Low Countries.

John II of Luxembourg, Count of Ligny (1392-1441): was a French nobleman and soldier, a younger son of John of Luxembourg, Lord of Beauvoir, and Marguerite of Enghien. He is remembered for leading the force that captured Joan of Arc at the Siege of Compiègne.

Joan, Countess of Saint-Pol and Ligny (died 1430). called the "Demoiselle de Luxembourg", she was the ruling Count of Saint Pol and Count of Ligny

---

[207] The Retrial of 1456. The English translation of the trial files from 1902. From the book: Jeanne d'Arc Maid of Orléans Deliverer of France. Edited by T. Douglas Murray, Deposition of Guillaume Colles, or Boisguillaume Priest, Notary Public.

in 1430. She was the daughter of Guy of Luxembourg, Count of Ligny and Mahaut of Châtillon, Countess of Saint-Pol. She did not marry and had no children. At the death of Philip I, Duke of Brabant, she was his nearest living relative on the Saint-Pol side and inherited Saint-Pol and Ligny upon his death. She was living at the time at the Castle Beaurevoir which belonged to her favorite nephew John. At this time, John held Joan of Arc as a prisoner. The Demoiselle de Luxembourg is remembered for showing kindness to Joan and pleaded with her nephew not to sell Joan to the English, giving him a promise to make him her heir if he did not. She died in 1430 and her nephew decided to sell Joan to the English.

Gratias In Aeternum[208]

Jesus, the Christ
By Rudolf Steiner, from the
"Representative of Humanity",
the Goetheanum, Dornach,
Switzerland.

The Archangel Michael
"Michael"
By Baron Arild von Rosenkrantz
(1870-1964).

Christian Rosenkreutz
"A Man in Armour", by
Rembrandt. This painting is
associated with CR by Rudolf
Steiner. He is also known as the
Count of St. Germain, Lazarus-
John, and the Knight of the Rose
Cross. He is a Great Initiate and
Leader of Humanity.

Dr. Rudolf Steiner
A Great Initiate, leader, and
founder of the Anthroposophical
Society in Dornach, Switzerland.
Photo circa June 1922, Vienna.

---

[208] "In Gratitude Eternally."

About the Author

As a seeker and researcher, the author is dedicated to exploring, as a lifetime journey, the mysteries of the spiritual worlds and humanity's connection as has been taught, documented, and shared publicly by a handful of genuine initiates, spiritual researchers, seekers, and teachers such as Rudolf Steiner ("Anthroposophy" and "Spiritual Science") including the works of supporting founders of the Anthroposophical Society. This lifelong pursuit is the study of the paths and the knowledge given to us by individuals who have bridged the gap, to whatever degree, between the physical and spiritual worlds.

The author earned a Master of Theology from Southern Methodist University and a Master of Business Administration from Baylor University; both with academic honors. He also earned a Bachelor of Arts degree in Economics from the University of North Texas.

The Author, Spring, 2020.

May the imprint of my life lead to a better existence for those who come in contact with this work. May those who are born on the earth plane during and after my ascension into the spiritual worlds benefit from the contents of this work. May this work lead them to the Christ.[209]

---

[209] Ex Deo Nascimur, Im Christo Morimur, Per Spiritum Reviviscimus. "Out of God I was born, In Christ I died, in the Holy Spirit I am reborn."